New Hampshire

OFF THE
BEATEN
PATH™

SECOND EDITION

BARBARA RADCLIFFE ROGERS
AND STILLMAN ROGERS

A Voyager Book

The Globe Pequot Press

Old Saybrook, Connecticut

S0-ACO-484

*To George Radcliffe and Norman Rogers, the fathers who
chose New Hampshire as our childhood home, and to
James C. Cleveland, who as a U.S. Congressman worked
so long and hard to preserve its character
and protect its land.*

Cover map © DeLorme Mapping
Illustrations by Carole Drong

Off the Beaten Path is a trademark of The Globe Pequot Press, Inc.

Library of Congress Cataloging-in-Publication Data
Rogers, Barbara Radcliffe.
  New Hampshire : off the beaten path / by Barbara Radcliffe Rogers
and Stillman Rogers. — 2nd ed.
    p.   cm. — (Off the beaten path series)
  "A Voyager book."
  Includes index.
  ISBN 1-56440-627-X
  1. New Hampshire—Guidebooks.   I. Rogers, Stillman, 1939–
  II. Title.   III. Series.
F32.3.R64   1994
917.4104'43—dc20   94-37251
                                                                CIP

Manufactured in the United States of America
Second Edition/First Printing

New Hampshire

OFF THE BEATEN PATH™

"A New Hampshire guidebook that will both entertain and inform New Hampshire natives and visitors alike. This book deserves a permanent home in the glove compartment of your car."
  —The Honorable Walter Peterson, former governor of New Hampshire and president of Franklin Pierce College

"Unusual places that are worth making a detour for."
  —*The Boston Globe*

"Hidden treasures unknown to many New Hampshire natives."
  —*Northeast Outdoors*

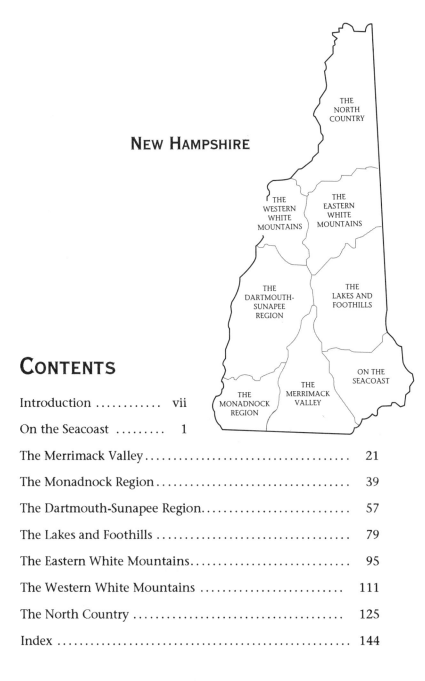

NEW HAMPSHIRE

THE NORTH COUNTRY

THE WESTERN WHITE MOUNTAINS

THE EASTERN WHITE MOUNTAINS

THE DARTMOUTH-SUNAPEE REGION

THE LAKES AND FOOTHILLS

ON THE SEACOAST

THE MONADNOCK REGION

THE MERRIMACK VALLEY

Contents

ACKNOWLEDGMENTS

Any book is a joint effort, but this one has profited from the help of friends and family all over New Hampshire—and from a number of others who were strangers when we began, but are now counted as friends.

They have shared with us their favorite off the beaten path places, those restaurants, inns, hiking trails, and back roads that even a traveler used to poking into all the corners might miss. Our gratitude goes to Joan Farrel, Judy Hampe, Chris Hamm, Joanne Lemieux, Ted and Elsie Miner, Pauline and Frank Mooney, Lee Stark, Larry Pletcher, Nina Gardner, Dennis and Sandy Brennan, Kathleen Hatt, Philip Hollman, Mike and Merri Hern, Joe Keenan, Ray Gorman, Betty Falton, Käthe Dillman, Art and Nancy Brennan, Doris Thibeault, Liz and Dennis Hagar, Michael Coyle, Trudy and Frank Cutrone, and Susan and Malcolm McLane.

Very special thanks go to Len Reed of Bethlehem for the hours he spent telling us about places we would never have found without him. It was Len who also suggested many of the wonderful inns that welcomed us after long days of travel, and which we, in turn, recommend in this book. Many more were suggested by Dick Hamilton, from his vast knowledge of the White Mountains that he so readily shared with us.

We have shared our travels over the years with many friends: hikes and backroads with Patty Hanson, mountain trails and fishing boats with Carole Belsky and John Norton, campfires with Fred and Sta Gursky, campsites with Mark and Marge Davis, and miles of trails above the timberline with Howard and Sue Poore. Possibly the most hilarious of these adventures we have shared with Frank and Maria Sibley, as we searched for gorges, boulders, and ghost towns. Julie and Lura have always been fun to travel with, whether we were slipping over rocky trails in search of a waterfall in a downpour of rain, or enjoying a leisurely second cup of tea at a Portsmouth bakery.

Our fondest appreciation goes to Dee Radcliffe, who has explored every corner of the state and whose notes and suggestions led us to places even the locals didn't know about. Her good humor and enthusiasm will always place her among life's best traveling companions.

INTRODUCTION

How do you introduce a friend, one with whom you've shared many of life's pleasures, one whose company never fails you? What can you possibly say of your friend that will capture those qualities that are most endearing and most enduring?

New Hampshire is that friend to us. The first memories of our childhoods are set here. The first ocean waves we played in broke on New Hampshire beaches; the first mountains we climbed, slopes and trails we skied—they were New Hampshire's. We've lived and traveled in many other parts of the world, but when asked a few days ago which of all the places that we've traveled is our favorite, we said in unison, and without second thought, New Hampshire.

The tremendous diversity of New Hampshire's landscapes makes it visually exciting and also provides a wide variety of activities, particularly for those who enjoy the outdoors. The challenges of its terrain, soil, and climate have given its people a unique character—or perhaps such a place has always attracted those of independent and self-sufficient spirit.

New Hampshire people do tend to be an independent lot; most of them say exactly what they think. Another disconcerting trait to those who don't know us well is that you can't always tell about us by our looks. The size of a person's fortune often bears no relation to the size of one's home or the make of one's car. It is often said of Boston ladies that they don't buy their hats; they have them. New Hampshire people are like that too. The beautiful farmhouse may be all that's left several generations later and may be kept up by a lot of hard work alone; the tiny cottage with the gate askew may be the home of a millionaire. We tend to live in what we have.

The same trait is true of restaurants, which is very confusing to the traveler used to decorator interiors and flashy exteriors. You can't always judge a restaurant by its cover, and very often the plainest place or the most staid of inns may have a chef who retired to the country from a four-star bastion of haute cuisine. Surprises are what New Hampshire is full of, and they make each day a happy adventure.

"Off the beaten path" is a relative thing. By most standards, the whole state is off the beaten path. There are only three areas that are congested by traffic even in the height of tourist season. If lodging is heavily booked during the most popular weeks, it is not because there are too many people here, but because resorts do not line our roads. Reservations are always a good idea during July and August and around the first week of October. Places such as Garfield Falls, which even many local people have not seen, require travel on unpaved roads. But none of these require four-wheel-drive vehicles, except in winter or early spring when some roads are muddy or not plowed.

Which brings us to the question of when to come. New Hampshire is a seasonal state, and each month has its attractions. The best time for you to explore the Granite State depends upon your tastes and interests. Winter is glorious, filled with crystal-cold days for skiing or snowshoeing across white meadows with clear views of mountains through leafless trees. Night brings the stars so close you can spot constellations you never saw before and is a good time for a sleigh ride and a blazing fire in the hearth. Snow covers all the hardscrabble farms and rock-filled fields, and the air is clear and smells of wood smoke. But if you like little museums or want to hike to waterfalls, winter is not the best season.

Spring is good for country walks and hikes. Sugar houses come briefly to life, shrouded in steam and smelling of sweet maple syrup. With the end of the sap run, spring wildflowers carpet the woodlands, and the view of the mountains is softened, but not obscured, by leaves the size of mouse ears. Spring peepers fill the evening air with chirping, and strawberry farms invite you to pick your own. A lot of the little places aren't open yet, but people in the ones that are have time to chat and tell you about local places. Bed and breakfast hosts have time to share a glass of sherry with you after dinner. Spring comes so fast that you can almost watch the apple blossoms unfold.

Summer is full of festivals celebrating almost everything from blueberries to zucchinis, and every little town has its historical society open. Days are long and not too hot to enjoy hikes and climbs. Lake shores and mountain brooks offer swimming.

After Labor Day, the weather is still summery, but there is a lull in the number of tourists until the end of the month. Farmers' markets are filled with produce and jars of glistening jellies. Hiking is at its very best, and the roadsides are brightened by patches of turning swamp maples.

Foliage paints the state, from north to south, in brilliant shades of red and gold. It begins in mid-September in the north country and lasts until mid- to late October in the Monadnock region. The peak can vary by a week or so, depending on the weather, but any area will have at least two weeks of good color, usually more.

So plan your travel dates according to your own interests, or better yet, come often and enjoy the best of each season.

Prices are a tricky thing to provide in a guide book, but we have done it anyway. They change with economic conditions, even seasons and weather conditions, since restaurants depend upon the markets for fresh produce and seafood. Lodging rates usually rise during the busiest times and drop during the slower ones. We have given dollar amounts when they seemed fairly likely to remain constant and elsewhere have used general ranges. For bed and breakfast places we consider $60.00 to $70.00 a night for two people to be moderate; for inns and hotels without breakfast, $70.00 to $85.00 is moderate. In restaurants, $10.00 to $20.00 is moderate for the main course, and we've further broken that into a high and low if the prices fall into a close range. How you add to that with other courses and wine will affect your bill, of course, but the entrée price sets the base. Sometimes we've been even more specific, especially if the prices are exceptional.

Now to all the usual disclaimers, the caveat emptor endemic to travel guides: Things change, especially in the restaurant business. We've tried to choose places with consistent ownership, but when we discover a great new spot, we can't wait five years to share it with you. If you find our recommendations not up to our descriptions, there are several possible reasons. The restaurant in question may have changed owners or chefs, or it may have just plain gone downhill. Your taste in food may not be the same as ours. One man's pâté is another's "ptoooi," as Confucius wisely observed. There is no substitute for your own good judgment. If you get inside and don't think it's the right place for you, leave. In those memorable cases where a place we've recommended doesn't look like what it tastes like, we've mentioned that fact so that you will expect it. If in doubt, don't be embarrassed to ask to see a menu before you're seated. New Hampshire people don't buy pigs in a poke and they don't expect you to either.

Enjoy New Hampshire as we do. We think that you'll agree after you've met the state in person that it's a place where familiarity breeds both respect and love.

> *The prices and rates listed in this guidebook were confirmed at press time. We recommend, however, that you call establishments to obtain current information before traveling.*

ABOUT THE AUTHORS

Barbara Radcliffe Rogers and Stillman Rogers have, jointly and singly, written and illustrated more than twenty-five books, most of them on travel, wildlife, and gardening. Titles include *Galapagos, Safari, The Portugal Traveler, Big Cats, Giant Pandas,* and *Exploring Europe by Boat.* They have written and illustrated several books in the *Children of the World* series describing the lives and cultures of children from Argentina to Zambia. Barbara has written articles for *Yankee* Magazine, *Country Journal, Animal Kingdom,* the *Los Angeles Times,* and others, including a column, "The Travel Advisor," for the *Walpole Gazette* in Walpole, New Hampshire. Stillman's photographs have illustrated these and other articles.

In *New Hampshire: Off The Beaten Path,* they write for the first time about their home state. Although they have explored its trails and back roads since childhood, they still find it as fascinating as the most exotic locales in their wide repertoire of travels.

ON THE SEACOAST

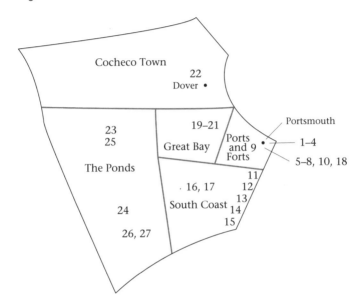

Cocheco Town

22
Dover •

23
25

The Ponds

19–21

Great Bay

Ports
and 9
Forts

Portsmouth

1–4

5–8, 10, 18

11
12
13
14

16, 17

South Coast

24

26, 27

15

1. Fort Constitution
2. Great Island Common
3. Fort Stark
4. Odiorne Point
5. Drisco House
6. The Abbott Grocery Store
7. Port of Portsmouth Maritime Museum
8. Wentworth-Coolidge Mansion
9. Urban Forestry Center
10. Isles of Shoals
11. Whale watches
12. Little Boar's Head
13. Fuller Gardens
14. Tuck Museum
15. The Science and Nature Center

16. Gilman Garrison House
17. American Independence Museum
18. Piscataqua River Cruises
19. The Little Bay Buffalo Company
20. Great Bay Estuarine Research Reserve
21. Emery Farm
22. Woodman Institute
23. Point of View Farm
24. Harlow's Bread and Cracker Company
25. Pawtuckaway Boulders
26. Sandown Depot Railroad Museum
27. Sandown Meeting House

ON THE SEACOAST

New Hampshire has the shortest seacoast of any coastal state, only 18 miles long, but it's also one of the most historic. The first European settlers established a settlement at Odiorne Point in 1623, and later the same year a fishing village was established at Dover Point on the northern banks of the Piscataqua River on Little Bay. The Odiorne Point settlement was abandoned, but the Dover settlers built a meeting house and homes, which became the first permanent settlement in the colony.

The histories of this area, the American colonies, and the young nation are inextricably intertwined. The first American flag to be saluted by a foreign power flew from the mast of the *Ranger,* which sailed from Portsmouth in 1777. The flag was sewn by Portsmouth ladies of fabric cut from their dresses. Portsmouth today, for all of its funky shops and bright eateries, still has the air of a prosperous eighteenth-century seaport.

Exeter, too, was a ship-building town and a lively port. Although it has now lost its navigable link with the sea, its fine buildings still speak of the profitable India trade. Inland from the shores of the Great Bay stretched almost unbroken farmland, and, although more heavily settled than other parts of the state, the area is still rich in farms and orchards.

Although most visitors' view of the New Hampshire coast is the traffic and commercialism of Route 1, there are lovely and quiet back roads to enjoy even in this playground area. Portsmouth, too, has its surprises, tucked away amid its tangle of old lanes and paths that grew into streets. New Hampshire, as a colony, began in this seacoast area, and it's an appropriate place for us to begin exploring the state.

PORTS AND FORTS

The link with the sea did not end with the sailing of the last clipper. Ships were built in Portsmouth for both world wars, and the forts that guarded the harbor in the Revolution still dot the coast.

New Castle, once called Great Island, was the first seat of government and even now looks like the tiny prosperous fishing and seafaring village of its colonial origins. Streets too narrow for sidewalks are lined with houses whose doorways open directly

Lighthouse at Fort Constitution

onto the roadway. The numbers on them are not addresses, but dates, most of them from the 1600s and 1700s.

◆ **Fort Constitution** had its beginning in 1632 with the earthworks and four "great guns"; a blockhouse was built in 1666, and at the end of the century a breastwork was built to protect the military stores. It was named Fort William and Mary.

Paul Revere, the Boston silversmith and patriot, is best known for his ride the night of April 18, 1775. But in New Hampshire, he's remembered for a ride almost four months earlier. On December 13, 1774, he brought a message that British troops were coming from Rhode Island to protect the garrison and

3

secure it against the fractious Sons of Liberty. The next day, 400 Sons of Liberty converged on the fort and liberated one hundred barrels of gunpowder and some small arms, which they loaded on a gundalow (a type of boat built at Portsmouth and used to navigate tidal rivers) and sailed up the Oyster River to Durham. They hid the gunpowder in homes and under the pulpit of the meetinghouse until they could haul it by ox cart to Cambridge for use at Bunker Hill. On December 15, before the British could get reinforcements, another group helped themselves to sixteen small cannon and whatever other military supplies they could carry off. It was the first active engagement of the Revolution.

Renamed Fort Constitution, it was used in 1812 and every other war until it was returned to the state of New Hampshire in 1961. Its walls and ramparts are a fine place for viewing the lighthouse, harbor, and Fort McClary, which guards the other side of this harbor entrance from Kittery Point, Maine. Visitors must observe the parking restrictions posted at the Coast Guard Station entrance. Open 8:00 A.M. to 4:30 P.M. daily.

For access to the rocks and sandy beach of the neighboring shore, go through ◆ **Great Island Common,** a park overlooking the harbor. From here you can see two lighthouses, islands, and Fort Constitution, as well as passing sailboats. Rocky tidal areas surround the park with pools to explore and a gentler tide than the one that crashes against the rocks along the ocean. While the beach isn't very long, it's set in a very attractive cove. The park provides picnic tables, a pavilion, and grills, as well as playgrounds, ballfields, and restrooms. There are no camping facilities. Open daily May to September until dark; admission is $2.00 per adult; seniors and children are free.

Close to this park, look for the entrance to Wild Rose Lane, which ends at ◆ **Fort Stark.** It is another of the seven forts built to protect Portsmouth Harbor and the naval shipyard. Although it was the site of earthworks during the Revolution and the War of 1812 and of a later stone fort, the present batteries were built at the turn of the century and were used in both world wars. Be careful as you climb around the batteries; a flashlight will be handy if you plan to explore inside. Look for the tracks in the ceiling of Battery Hunter where ammunition was moved from the magazine and hoisted through a hole in the ceiling to the enormous guns in their emplacements above. The huge steel doors of the magazines stand ajar, grass grows from the cement, and one round gun emplacement has begun to slide down the crumbling cliff. Open Saturday and Sunday 10:00 A.M. to 5:00 P.M. between Memorial Day and Labor Day.

Facing New Castle Island and Fort Stark is ✦ **Odiorne Point,** where the first Europeans in the state settled. Site of Fort Dearborn during World War II, the grass-covered hills are actually camouflaged bunkers for gun emplacements and their support systems. The entire point is now a nature center, with diverse coastal habitats to explore. Along with the rocky shore and salt marsh, there are a freshwater marsh and coastal woods. A drowned forest of pine, birch, and hemlock stumps is firmly rooted about two feet below tide level at the south end. Throughout the natural habitat you can see signs of human habitation as well. Stone walls of old farmlands and a colony of summer cottages cross the area, and you may see the hardy remnants of some of the formal gardens of the long-gone cottages. The only one of these now standing is the Seacoast Science Center. Programs and tours on such varied subjects as wild shore edibles, sea legends, coastal defenses, whales, marshes, and geology are conducted by the New Hampshire Audubon Society and the University of New Hampshire Marine Science Program. The center offers activities for children, including a day camp program. Open daily, mid-May to mid-October, 8:00 A.M. to 8:00 P.M. A small entry fee is charged. Write P.O. Box 674, Rye 03870 or call (603) 436–8043 (off-season 603–862–3460). For information on special programs call (603) 862–1088.

Portsmouth is a lively city with warrens of back streets to explore. The path to its abundant historic homes is so well beaten that a red line is painted on the sidewalks indicating **"The Portsmouth Trail."** But these are not the only interesting or historic places to visit in Portsmouth.

The original name for the settlement here was **Strawbery Banke,** after the river banks red with the fruit in the late spring. A restoration preserving nearly four centuries of this old waterfront neighborhood, saved from demolition in the 1950s, now uses the name Strawbery Banke. Thirty of the thirty-five historic homes here stand on their original foundations. The unusual feature of the restoration is that instead of returning the neighborhood to any single period and showing what things looked like then, the buildings and their furnishings show the evolution of homes, gardens, shops, and daily life throughout the entire period of its existence.

The most dramatic example of this whole-history approach is at the ◆ **Drisco House,** built in 1795. The house changed with the times, and when it was acquired, one side of the duplex was a "frozen in time" 1950s apartment. It has been saved as it stood, but the other half of the house has been restored to its origins as the store and home of an eighteenth-century mid-level tradesman. This, too, is unusual, for the homes that are usually saved and restored are those of wealthy and prominent citizens— homes far more elegant and ornate than the Drisco House. This one building, with its 1795 and 1955 halves, spans the history of the Puddle Dock neighborhood in Portsmouth.

The process of discovery and restoration is a continuing one, and visitors are invited to share in it through a number of exhibits showing cut-away walls and structural details. The **Joshua Jackson and Sherburn houses** are dedicated entirely to old house archaeology, showing not only how the homes were built, but also how historians can detect the changes made over the centuries. To anyone restoring an older home, looking inside the mechanics of original and renovated construction is an invaluable lesson. To the more casual visitor, it's just plain interesting.

Portsmouth was a major shipyard during World War II, and life on the home front in a coastal city is illustrated at ◆ **The Abbott Grocery Store,** restored to its 1943 appearance and contents. The storekeeper's apartment next door and exhibits in the rear of the building all show how life on the homefront changed during the war.

For more than fifty years the family of a New Hampshire governor of the Civil War era lived in the **Goodwin Mansion,** and his wife's detailed and spirited diaries provide information that has made it possible to restore not only the house, but her remarkable gardens as well. At various times in the summer and fall, Victorian teas are served in these gardens.

Without major endowment, Strawbery Banke continues to grow as funds are available, usually from local donations or entry fees. It is exciting to watch the restorations take place, and each visit gives a dimension of being part of its progress. Even the gifts purchased at the **Dunaway Store,** the museum's shop, help fund the restoration. It's like giving twice when you do your Christmas shopping there.

Speaking of Christmas, on the first two weekends of December, the village opens for a **Candlelight Stroll.** Candles light the windows as you wander through the streets with costumed carolers and musicians. The houses are decorated for the holidays and offer free refreshments to visitors. Craftspeople are at work, and you can shop for gifts in their workshops or in the museum stores. Each year brings new features, and it's an occasion for local people to enjoy the uncrowded winter quiet of Strawbery Banke. The stroll takes place on four evenings only, from 4:30 to 8:30 P.M., and costs $8.00 for adults and $4.00 for children ages ten to sixteen (younger children are admitted free).

The restored buildings are open daily 10:00 A.M. to 5:00 P.M. from May 1 through October 31. A two-day admission pass is $10.00 for adults, $7.00 for ages six to seventeen, and free for children under age six. Write Strawbery Banke, Marcy Street, P.O. Box 300, Portsmouth 03802 or call (603) 433–1100.

Gardeners should stop at **Prescott Park** across the street to see the All America Show Garden, where each year's All America selections are grown. Show gardens such as this are located in different parts of the country to demonstrate which flowers perform best in various climates. Northerners who spot boxwood at Strawbery Banke may wonder how it grows in New Hampshire. The answer is that Portsmouth and a tiny coastal strip are in a different gardening zone from the rest of the state, due to the moderating effect of the sea.

Built at the Portsmouth Naval Shipyard in 1953, the *Albacore*, now at the ◆ **Port of Portsmouth Maritime Museum,** never went to war. Her mission was an experimental one, as she was planned to be redesigned and adapted as the prototype for the submarine of the future. The teardrop hull design made her the fastest submarine ever put in the water. That and dive brakes, sonar systems, and other new theories tested on board have become part of modern submarine design. The fascinating story of this experimental submarine and how its fifty-five-member crew lived in its 205-foot by 27-foot confines during its nineteen years of commission is told during a ten-minute video and a half-hour tour of the vessel. Now sunk in a dry basin so you can see the entire hull, the USS *Albacore* looks a bit like a beached whale

7

up close. It's the only one of its kind, so if the sea and its ships interest you at all, don't pass up the chance to see it. Open 9:30 A.M. to 4:30 P.M. every day; the last tour begins at 4:00 P.M. Adults $4.00, seniors $3.00, children ages seven to twelve $2.00, families $10.00. You'll find the *Albacore* on the Market Street Extension, or Route 1 bypass. Write 600 Market Street, Portsmouth 03801 or call (603) 436–3680.

With all of the things to do in Portsmouth, you are sure to be looking for a place to eat by now. There are plenty to choose from, since downtown Portsmouth has more restaurants in a smaller area than any other part of New Hampshire. Everyone has a few favorites, so we'll tell you ours. **The Bagelry** at 19 Market Street has outstanding breakfast bagels and lunch or snack sandwiches (603–431–5853). **Ceres Bakery,** at 51 Penhallow Street, bakes incomparable breads, cookies, tortes, and coffee cakes. Nowhere else will you find such generous slices of the last two served up for $1.00 to $1.50. Hearty thick soups are served with a slice of their daily bread, or you can choose quiches or salads. Lunch with dessert will be under $5.00. It opens at 5:30 A.M. for travelers who like to be on the road early (603–431–6518).

You could easily pass right by **Karen's** without noticing it was a restaurant, with its curtained windows and side entrance off a narrow lane. The interior has the air of a country café, with painted vines trailing around the doors and fireplace. A good selection of dishes includes a creamy, but not heavy, crabmeat Alfredo, pan-blackened swordfish with peach chutney, and chicken in a garlic mustard sauce. They serve lunch daily, dinner Tuesday through Saturday, at 105 Daniel Street (603–431–1948).

Within walking distance from Strawbery Banke and most of the other attractions of Portsmouth, the **Bow Street Inn** occupies the top floor of a harborside building that once housed a brewery. Tastefully decorated rooms with queen-size brass beds frame views of the harbor; breakfast breads are homemade and the hospitable innkeepers take time to suggest restaurants, activities, and their own favorite corners of Portsmouth. The inn is at 121 Bow Street, Portsmouth 03801; call (603) 431–7760.

On the inland side of the downtown area, the **Sise Inn** has a more hotel-like atmosphere, but in the elegant surroundings of a prosperous Portsmouth merchant's home. Breakfast is do-it-yourself in the large, bright dining room, refitted with a small kitchen at one side. Rooms are spacious and stylish; prices begin at over $100. Located at 40 Court Street, Portsmouth 03801; telephone (603) 433–1200.

Out of town, where the Little Harbor Road ends at the water's edge, is the ❖ **Wentworth-Coolidge Mansion.** It is one of very few residences of a royal governor virtually unchanged since the Revolution. The governor lived well. The home that he built in 1750 was originally even larger and was the most elegant of its day. It was not only his residence, but the center of government as well. You can tour the original rooms and the Governor's Council Chamber, where he signed the charters for land grants and towns throughout New Hampshire and Vermont. The grounds, where you are welcome to picnic, are planted with the first lilacs brought to the New World. They are the state flower, and if you visit New Hampshire in May you will see them blooming in dooryards, gardens, and at the sites of long-deserted farms throughout the countryside. Although technically an "exotic" here, lilacs have a long history in the state and have been accepted as native. Open from 10:00 A.M. to 5:00 P.M. from Memorial Day to Labor Day. (Perhaps this is a good place to mention that Memorial Day in New Hampshire is still observed on May 30, not the nearest Monday.) The Wentworth-Coolidge Mansion is on Little Harbor Road, off Route 1A in Portsmouth (603–436–6607).

South of Portsmouth, not far from Route 1, is the 150-acre property of the ❖ **Urban Forestry Center.** A beautiful place to visit for its gardens, woodland, and salt marsh landscapes, it is also an attractive demonstration area whose purpose is not only to protect this piece of land, but to show others how they can protect and enhance their own property as well. Individuals, municipalities, developers, and conservation commissions all look to the center for inspiration and advice. Throughout the property are mailboxes where you will find extensive information on each project. Plant-by-plant descriptions are available at the perennial border, and a thorough booklet on herb culture and uses, prepared by Tanya Jackson (one of New England's leading herb experts), is free at the herb garden. The Center sponsors lectures, field trips, and programs on natural history, wildlife, gardening, and New Hampshire forests. Most of the programs are on Thursday evenings and cost a modest $2.00 admission.

A "Garden for the Senses," created especially for the visually and physically impaired, emphasizes plants selected for flavor, fragrance, color, and texture, with wide paths and raised beds for easy access. An arboretum contains examples of trees for street plantings, cold-hardy trees, and those with unusual and interesting flowers, bark, or leaves. Several plantations and trails as well as ample space for watching birds that live in the marsh and shore areas add to the Center's attractions. Free and open year-round, the trails are favorites of cross-country skiers and snow-shoe hikers (no motorized recreational vehicles). Hours are 7:00 A.M. to dusk daily. The office is open 8:00 A.M. to 4:00 P.M. Monday through Friday. The Center is at 45 Elwyn Road (off Lafayette Road) in Portsmouth; call (603) 431–6774 for more information.

Off the coast, shared with Maine, but with access from New Hampshire, and visible only in clear weather, are the ◆ **Isles of Shoals.** Described by the writer and poet Celia Thaxter, who grew up there, they were painted by the impressionist artist Childe Hassam, who came to the summer arts colony that developed there. His work includes over 400 paintings of the islands, many of which were done to illustrate Thaxter's *An Island Garden,* a classic of garden writing as fresh in its facsimile reprint as it was at its original printing at the turn of the century. These islands are as wrapped in tales of shipwrecks, pirates, ghosts, and buried treasure as they are in fog. Craggy and barren as they were when Captain John Smith called them "barren piles of rock," the islands still fascinate visitors. The Isles of Shoals Steamship Company at 315 Market Street will take passengers to Star Island for a three-hour shore visit. Write them at P.O. Box 311, Portsmouth 03801 or call (603) 431–5500. Whale watching, fishing, harbor, and Great Bay cruises out of Portsmouth are also offered by Portsmouth Harbor Cruises at Ceres Street Dock, 64 Ceres Street, Portsmouth 03801 (603–436–8084 or 800–776–0915).

THE SOUTH COAST

The shoreline in Rye is less developed than elsewhere, with long stretches of open saltmarsh (some of it a wildlife preserve), and rocky coast broken by beaches. New Hampshire Seacoast Cruises operates boat trips from Rye Harbor including day and evening ❖ **whale watches** and two-hour **cruises to the Isles of Shoals.** For information write to them at P.O. Box 232, Rye 03870 or call (603) 964–5545. Atlantic Fishing Fleet offers deep-sea fishing trips and whale watches on board *Atlantic Queen II* from April through mid-October. For a schedule write to P.O. Box 678, Rye Harbor 03870 or telephone (603) 964–5220.

Overlooking the ocean is **Saunders at Rye Harbor,** a local institution for more than seventy years. The menu offers a wider range of dishes than you would expect in a restaurant best known for its lobster. Seafood-stuffed mushroom caps, herbed toasted pita points, Jamaican scampi plus five "healthy choices," including chicken Marsala, highlight the menu. On Route 1A: call (603) 964–6466.

The outstanding Italian menu at **Cafe Avellino** mixes robust country foods with the most sophisticated classics. The shellfish, especially the mussels, are delectable; vegetables are treated with respect. Portions are very large, unusual for a restaurant of Avellino's style and elegance. Local food lovers get a faraway look in their eyes at the mention of this place, so be sure to call for reservations during busy seasons. They serve dinner daily from 5:00 P.M. and brunch on Sunday from 11:00 A.M. until 3:00 P.M. Cafe Avellino is at 1667 Ocean Blvd. in Rye Beach; (603) 427–2453.

For a shorebound excursion that gives you nature on one side and human nature on the other, walk or bicycle around ❖ **Little Boar's Head.** A 2-mile path goes along the ridge of a rocky promontory, with waves crashing on the rocks below. Inland stands a row of beach "cottages" built in the pre–income tax days when wealthy city dwellers moved their families and household staffs to the shore for the summer. In the early summer wild roses bloom along the path.

Roses at ❖ **Fuller Gardens** are clearly not wild: 1,500 carefully tended rosebushes thrive in the sea air in an All America Rose Display Garden, once part of a fine old Boar's Head estate. Both roses and perennial beds are at their peak in June, but the gardens are filled with blooms all summer and late into the fall. Don't miss the gate in the hedge leading to the cool, cedar-shaded Japanese garden with its pool, bridge, and stone lantern. Marble walkways surround a terraced formal garden. Open 10:00 A.M. to 6:00 P.M. daily during blooming season, the gardens are on

Fuller Gardens

Willow Avenue, which leaves Route 1A just north of its intersection with Route 101D, in North Hampton. The telephone is (603) 964–5414. Admission is $3.50.

The town of Hampton lies inland, out of hearing distance of raucous Hampton Beach. Follow Park Avenue east from Route 1 to find the original settlement at Meetinghouse Green. The old common is now a memorial park to the first settlers, with a stone for each of the pioneer families put there by their descendants. Across the street is the ◆**Tuck Museum,** operated by the Hampton Historical Society, a group of buildings that includes an old one-room schoolhouse, a museum of early farm implements, the Seacoast Fire Museum, and a variety of exhibits on the area's history. It isn't the Smithsonian but it is a very approachable collection; most items are not in glass cases but right where you can see them. A playground on the shady lawn outside will amuse the children if your attention span exceeds theirs. Open 1:00 to 4:00 P.M. Thursday through Sunday from mid-June to mid-September. Admission is free. The museum is at 40 Park Avenue, Hampton 03842; call (603) 929–0781 for news of special events.

On Route 84 in Hampton Falls is the **Raspberry Farm,** where you can pick a quart or two of sweet juicy berries in a few minutes from vines trellised to protect your arms from bramble scratches. You can also buy berries already picked or cooked into delectable jams and jellies. There is always freshly churned homemade raspberry ice cream in the freezer, as tempting as the fresh berries themselves. Open throughout the summer and into October, noon to 5:00 P.M. Monday to Friday and 9:00 A.M. to 5:00 P.M. Saturday and Sunday. Call (603) 926–6604 for more information.

◆ **The Science and Nature Center** at New Hampshire Yankee, the area's power station, explores the various sources of energy and their effects on the environment. Hands-on exhibits, such as a bicycle-powered generator (how long can you keep the light burning?) and computerized quizzes, fill the science center, and an aquarium shows local marine life. The Oascoag nature trail winds through woods and marshlands where markers explain the habitats, natural history, and plant life. Shorebirds abound, and muskrats, foxes, rabbits, and woodchucks may wander within sight if you are quiet. Such salt marshes are important sources of food and breeding grounds for wildlife, as well as providing filtration areas to keep groundwater pure. Open Mondays through Saturdays, except holidays, 9:00 A.M. to 4:00 P.M. Closed Saturdays in the winter; free admission. Write Seabrook Station, Route 1, Seabrook 03874 or call (603) 474–9521 or (800) 338–7482.

If you're staying in the area with children, they'll enjoy the petting farm at the Best Western **Seabrook Inn.** There's quite an assortment: rabbits and sheep, white doves and llamas, even a cow the kids can learn to milk and a pony to ride. The inn is at 9 Stard Road, Seabrook 03874; telephone (603) 474–3078.

Exeter, like Portsmouth, is a nice place for walking. Fine homes line its streets, and three of the finest Federal mansions face the bandstand in the center of town. The ◆ **Gilman Garrison House** was built of massive hewn logs in the late 1600s as a fortified garrison. In the mid-1700s the house was enlarged and remodeled, adding a wing and more formal rooms in which its owner felt more comfortable entertaining John Wentworth, the royal governor, during his visits to Exeter. These visits ended abruptly when the governor had to take refuge in Fort William and Mary and finally flee altogether at the outbreak of the Revolution. (Since Portsmouth was considered a hotbed of Toryism, the seat of the state's government moved to Exeter—making it the state's first capital.) Later, Daniel Webster boarded in this house while he was a student at Phillips Exeter Academy. Open June 1 to October 1, Tuesday, Thursday, Saturday, and Sunday, noon to 5:00 P.M. The Gilman Garrison House is at the corner of Water and Clifford streets in Exeter; call (603) 436–3205.

Also in the center of town is the ◆ **American Independence Museum,** a newly established combination of the Ladd-Gilman House (home of New Hampshire's governor during the Revolution) and the Folsom Tavern, with the archives of the Society of the Cincinnati. The collections in the two eighteenth-century buildings feature furnishings from the 1600s, two annotated drafts of the U.S. Constitution, and historic artifacts. Escorted tours are given Wednesday through Sunday afternoons (the last tour begins at 4:00), May through October. Located at One Governor's Lane (off Center Street), Exeter 03833; telephone (603) 772–0861.

Art Deco enthusiasts should stop at the **Ioka Theater** in downtown Exeter, where the lobby has been restored to its 1915 origins and the soda fountain serves floats and phosphates. Classic films are a specialty here. The soda fountain is open 11:00 A.M. to 5:30 P.M. daily (603–772–2222).

Known best to students, parents, and alumni of Phillips Exeter Academy, **The Inn of Exeter** offers a wide variety of rooms that retain the charm of a historic hotel while providing modern and stylish lodgings. Antiques accent the spacious lobby, which sets the hotel's tone of unstuffy elegance. The dining room scores high, even in the seacoast area's abundance of good restaurants. Favorite entrées are given new life with carefully chosen accompaniments—tournedos of beef paired with apricots and pistachios, for example—and each dish is prepared with meticulous attention to detail. The restaurant is busy during special

14

events at the Academy, so call ahead to be sure of a table. The inn is at the corner of Front and Pine streets, Exeter 03833; telephone (603) 772–5901 or (800) 782–8444.

GREAT BAY

Past Portsmouth harbor, the Piscataqua River opens into Little Bay, which is fed by the Oyster River and **Great Bay.** At 5 miles long, Great Bay is the largest inland body of salt water in New England, but it's very hard to see since only one road, Route 4, passes within sight. Even that allows views of only the northern end. The towns that lie along the rivers feeding it are all far from its tidal shores.

The best way to see this area is from the water, on a ◆ **Piscataqua River cruise,** a three-hour trip from Portsmouth to Durham, with a stop at the site of the Bickford Garrison to learn how it was defended in 1694 by one farmer who cleverly changed coats and voices to make the post seem well-manned. The tour includes a buffalo farm (see below) and a chance to sample a buffalo burger as well. Offered on weekends in the fall, when the foliage along the wooded shores is at its best, cruises are run by Isles of Shoals Steamship Co., 315 Market Street, P.O. Box 311, Portsmouth 03802; telephone (603) 431–5500 or (800) 894–5509 in New Hampshire, (800) 441–4620 outside the state.

◆ **The Little Bay Buffalo Company** is a family-run farm on rolling meadows and woodlands extending to the waters of Little Bay. It is habitat for a number of wildlife species and a migratory stop for waterfowl. The bison here are not for petting; they are usually visible in the pasture, often at close range. Also at the farm are displays on the interrelationship between the bison and the Indians' way of life, as well as information on local Indians who camped here in the summer to fish and hunt. A Company Store sells buffalo meat, hides, and related products such as buffalo tooth necklaces. The clear message here, well stated by the Langley family, is that using resources requires responsibility. To reach the farm, take Durham Point Road from Route 108 and watch for the small sign on Langley Road to the left. Open daily mid-April through late November, 9:00 A.M. to 5:00 P.M.; observation area open until sunset. 50 Langley Road, Durham 03824; telephone (603) 868–3300.

15

Durham is best known for the **University of New Hampshire,** which dominates the town and brings it to life. Beside Thompson Hall on the campus is a lovely ravine filled in May with lilacs of every shade from white to dark purple.

Off Durham Point Road, on the way to Newmarket, is the ◆ **Great Bay Estuarine Research Reserve,** more than 4,000 acres of tidal waters, mud flats, salt marsh, tidal creek woodlands, fields, and meadows on Adams Point. There is no nature center or organized visitor program here, but the habitat is filled with the flora and fauna peculiar to tidal estuaries. A boat put-in and parking area are reached by a stone-wall bordered road that ends at the Jackson Laboratory, an estuarine research center. Park there to reach the viewing platform (handicapped accessible) overlooking rolling meadows with the bay in the background. The air is filled with the trills of birds. For information on the Great Bay Reserve, call (603) 868–1095.

◆ **Emery Farm** was established in 1655, which, eleven generations later, makes it high on the list of the nation's oldest family farms. Here you can pick your own strawberries, blueberries, or raspberries. Juicy tree-ripened peaches and garden produce as well as local maple syrup, honey, and fresh home-baked breads are sold; New Hampshire crafts and pottery add to the unique farmstand. In the spring they sell herb plants and garden flats from their greenhouse. The farm is open every day, Easter through Christmas Eve (they also sell Christmas trees) from 9:00 A.M. to 6:00 P.M. Emery Farm is on Route 4, 2 miles east of Durham (603–742–8495).

COCHECO TOWN

Dover was the scene of repeated Indian attacks during the early years of the settlement, so nearly all of its garrison houses were destroyed. The only one still surviving is the 1765 **Damm Garrison,** which is protected by a roofed lattice portico between two brick buildings of the ◆ **Woodman Institute.** In original condition, this heavy log structure houses a collection of early furnishings and implements. The two exhibition buildings of the Woodman Institute are a tribute to the inquiring minds of the Victorians who assembled their contents. The collection of mounted animals contains specimens of most of the mammals native to the state and many, such as an 8-foot-tall polar bear,

16

that are not. In addition to an extensive collection of rocks, minerals, and lepidoptera, the museum displays fine examples of Sioux beadwork. President Lincoln's saddle, used in his last review of troops and inherited by his aide Colonel Daniel Hall after the assassination, highlights the Civil War collection on the third floor. The Hale House contains fine antique furniture and a variety of collections from the nineteenth century. Open Tuesday through Saturday, 2:00 to 5:00 P.M., at The Woodman Institute, 182 Central Avenue, Dover 03820, call (603) 742–1038.

Salmon Falls Stoneware is a potters' studio where they make salt-glazed stoneware and decorate it by hand with traditional designs. It is open daily, 9:00 A.M. to 5:00 P.M. You can find Salmon Falls Stoneware in the old Boston and Maine Engine House on Oak Street in Dover (603–749–1467).

Dover is a good place to use as a base while visiting the seacoast area. Quieter than Portsmouth or the beach towns, it is easier to find lodging here, especially in the summer. **Highland Farm** is a gracious bed and breakfast in a large mid–nineteenth-century brick home set in seventy-five acres of riverside meadow. Rooms are bright and large with either queen-size or double beds and are reached from a broad central hallway and an elegant double staircase. Breakfast, served in a formal dining room, features fresh fruit and homemade muffins or scones in addition to the main dish. The setting is so quiet and lovely that it's tempting to forget sightseeing entirely and enjoy the walking or cross-country ski trails along the river, the gardens, badminton and lawn games, or the hammock on the wide porch shaded by the mulberry tree full of birds. Write Highland Farm, 148 County Farm Road, Dover 03820 or call (603) 743–3399.

THE PONDS

Rides in fine restored carriages, sleighs, and wagons at ◆ **Point of View Farm** are more than transportation; they are, as owner Tyke Frost puts it, an "attempt to recapture some of the elegance that was part of the nineteenth century." Carriage rides are $15.00 per person (ages 12 and under $10.00). For a romantic evening Sue Frost prepares a full-course dinner after the carriage ride (with the coachman in top hat and tails) and serves it on antique china in a private Victorian dining room. Brunch combined with a surrey ride is $50.00 per couple. The Gathering Room is designed for birthday parties and other groups to have cake and ice cream after a hay or sleigh ride. Individual weekend rates are $5.00, $3.50 for children, and group rates start at $35.00 for a wagon or sleigh that holds fifteen or more people. Open year-round, reservations are required for special programs and are appreciated for individual and family visits. The farm is at 160 South Road, Deerfield 03074; telephone (603) 463–7974.

At ◆ **Harlow's Bread and Cracker Company,** in Epping, you can sample and buy scrumptious, not-so-traditional crackers; pizza, spicy cheddar, cracked pepper and ugly (blue cheese–based) to name just a few. Harlow's breads are equally delicious, and you can assemble a fine picnic with a creamy quiche, a delectable calzone, or a delicate focaccia. Don't leave without one of their delicious fig Newton bars, made from the Kennedy Bakery's original recipe. These are like nothing that ever came out of a box. This unusual bakery is on Route 27 within sight of Route 125. Write for their brochure (with mouth-watering descriptions of their crackers, which they ship), to 8 Exeter Road, Epping 03042, or call (603) 679–8883.

With the picnic basket freshly stocked from Harlow's, your next stop should be Pawtuckaway State Park. Along with its picnic area, this large park has both boat and canoe launch areas on the lake, two campgrounds with tent sites, a beach, and several hiking trails. One of these leads to the ◆ **Pawtuckaway Boulders,** a forest filled with huge glacial erratics that were broken from the cliffs on the two small mountains nearby and carried by the glacier to their present location a few thousand feet away in a valley to the east. The boulders vary in size, with some as long as 60 feet and over 30 feet high. Paths also lead to the summits of the three small mountains, two of which offer open views to the south. The campgrounds are open from late May to Columbus Day. Write Pawtuckaway State Park, RFD #1, Raymond 03077; call (603) 895–3301.

The ◆ **Sandown Depot Railroad Museum** is housed in a restored 1873 railroad station. It is thought to have been the busiest single-line railroad line in the country, with eighteen freight and sixteen passenger trains passing through Sandown each day. Most of the original railroad equipment is still in place, including the telegraph office. Open June through October,

Saturday and Sunday, 1:00 to 5:00 P.M. Admission is free. The museum is on Route 121A in Sandown; call (603) 887-4621 for more information.

Inquire at the museum to see if the ◆ **Sandown Meeting House** is open to visitors. Built in 1773 and 1774, it is the finest and best-preserved church structure in the state. It still has its original hand-wrought hinges and latches on the paneled doors, as well as the square pews and slave gallery. (It surprises many to learn that owning slaves was a fairly common practice among wealthier New England families—although never to the extent it was in the South.) The pulpit is goblet-shaped, with a canopy that acts as a sounding board. If you are interested in early construction techniques, ask to see the loft, reached by a ladder from the gallery. Cross beams are staggered, and mortised joints are held by wooden keys. According to a local tale the church took longer to construct than was anticipated and the rum supply ran out. The workmen refused to continue until the supply was replenished.

Bed-and-breakfast accommodation is surprisingly rare in this part of the state, so visitors are happy to discover **Stillmeadow B&B,** one of several well-restored mid–nineteenth-century homes on Route 121 in Hampstead. Rooms are moderately priced, warm and welcoming, with private baths, nicely chosen color schemes, and pleasant views. Breakfast is served with elegance in the dining room and features home-baked breads and muffins. Write to P.O. Box 565, Hampstead 03841 or call (603) 329-8381. The manicured lawns of the Hampstead Croquet Association are adjacent; Stillmeadow is a popular lodging during tournaments. The Association welcomes croquet enthusiasts as members.

THE MERRIMACK VALLEY

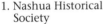

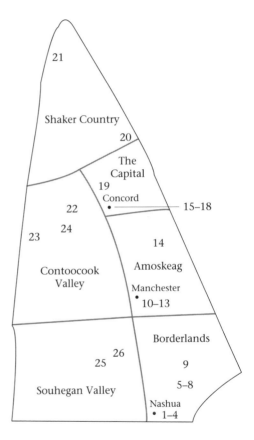

1. Nashua Historical Society
2. Abbot-Spaulding House
3. Mine Falls Park Heritage Trail
4. Ya Mama's
5. Robert Frost Homestead
6. Taylor Up and Down Sawmill
7. Derry Fire Department Museum
8. Upper Village National Historic District (Derry)
9. Chester Village Cemetery
10. Lawrence L. Lee Scouting Museum
11. Manchester Historical Association
12. Currier Gallery of Art
13. Amoskeag Fishway
14. Public archery ranges
15. New Hampshire Historical Society
16. Kimball-Jenkins Estate
17. Silk Farm Wildlife Sanctuary
18. St. Paul's School
19. Conservation Center (SPNHF)
20. Shaker Village
21. Tilton Arch
22. Fragrance Shop
23. Pat's Peak
24. St. Andrew's Episcopal Church
25. Beaver Brook Farm and Transportation Museum
26. Frye's Measure Mill

THE MERRIMACK VALLEY

While the seaport provided the early links that built Portsmouth and Exeter, the size and force of the Merrimack River as it gathered waters from rivers and mountain streams in the north provided power for manufacturing that built the valley cities. Towns sprang up around the mills, and they continued to grow together. Manchester, the state's largest city, grew with the largest cotton-mill complex ever built. Even today, long after the mighty Amoskeag mills closed their doors, the remaining mill buildings continue to dominate the city's riverbank.

This swath up the center of the state is flatter than the land to the north or the west, and is characterized by rolling hills, small lakes, and a surprising amount of open space, especially north of Manchester.

The Merrimack Valley has never been tourist country. Most visitors pass through it on their way to the pleasures of the lakes and mountains farther north. Concord is occasionally visited for its historical sites, but Manchester's rich ethnic cultures are largely unnoticed.

BORDERLANDS

Although it is the state's second largest city, Nashua is as rarely explored as the back roads that surround it. An early manufacturing city, it retains much of its millyard area and the canal that provided the 36-foot vertical drop needed to run the machinery. This history, as well as life in Nashua during the industrial era, is well illustrated in the museum of the ◆**Nashua Historical Society.** Changing exhibits feature subjects ranging from the role of Nashua in wars since the Civil War (arranged with interpretive and background information, as well as artifacts) to the interior of a local dry-goods store. Children will enjoy the schoolroom and the player piano. Open year-round, Tuesday, Wednesday, Thursday, and Saturday afternoons. The museum is at 5 Abbott Street, just off Route 101A (Amherst Street), Nashua 03063; telephone (603) 883–0015.

Next door, and also owned by the Historical Society, is the elegant ◆**Abbot-Spaulding House,** a Federal-style home built by the "Father of Nashua," Daniel Abbot. Both Daniel Webster and Franklin Pierce were frequent guests here; the furnishings were collected by the later owners and include several originals by designer Dexter Spaulding, as well as the family's collection of Sandwich glass. Although the Spauldings added some decorative details that were not there when the Abbots owned it, these are historically correct to the period and style of a leading family of the time. Open the same days as the museum next door.

For a view of Nashua's canal, walk the ◈ **Mine Falls Park Heritage Trail.** The path borders the river and canal, forming a loop that can be reached from Riverside Street, where there is ample parking. A put-in on Mill Pond gives canoes and small boats access to the canal. You can also reach the trail from the Millyard in downtown Nashua. For a trail map, contact the Nashua Conservation Commission at the City Hall, 229 Main Street, Nashua 03061.

We'll use any excuse to go to Nashua just to have a chance to eat at ◈ **Ya Mama's,** a tiny piece of Italy hiding behind a Canal Street storefront. Having eaten our way through their entire menu, we've never hit a bad night or a dish that disappointed. The peppers Palermo, a bright plateful of roasted red peppers with garlic and provolone, or the lumache agi olio (snails served without their shells) are good beginnings, as is the suppa di pesche, a steaming bowl of seafood in a savory broth frequently offered in the winter. Ya Mama's is at 42 Canal Street, Nashua 03061. Telephone (603) 883–2264.

The ◈ **Robert Frost Homestead** on Route 28 was the home of the poet for the first decade of this century. Frost credited the years that he spent at this Derry farm with shaping his future by providing him with time and seclusion. The simple 1880s farmhouse, the barn, the brook, orchards, and stone walls mentioned in his poems are all here, much as they were during his time. A nature trail labeled with lines of his poetry winds through meadow and forest. Open daily mid-June to Labor Day and weekends only Memorial Day to mid-June and Labor Day to Columbus Day. Telephone 603–432–3091.

Although sawmills are not rare in New Hampshire, the ◈ **Taylor Up and Down Sawmill** is the only up-and-down mill still operating. It is water-powered, with gears made of wood. The mill runs on Saturdays in July and August and four other days; ask for dates if you are interested in seeing it. Write Ballard State Forest, Island Pond Road, Derry 03038 or call (603) 271–3457.

23

Robert Frost Homestead

On the first floor of the old fire station on Main Street is the ✦ **Derry Fire Department Museum,** with old photos, vintage lifesaving and firefighting equipment, and an old industrial pumper from a local mill. Look for the poem Robert Frost wrote for the Derry Fire Department after he lost control of a grass fire on his farm. Upstairs, collections of the **Derry Historical Society** cover subjects ranging from the local witch hazel, shoe, and egg industries to native son and astronaut Allan Shepard. Robert Frost is, of course, featured here. The museum is open either Saturday or Sunday on summer weekends, and by prior arrangement at other times. Call (603) 432–3188 for information.

The village of East Derry, a short detour on the way to the Taylor Sawmill, was the original settlement in 1719; today several fine old buildings, including the Village Hall, comprise the ✦ **Upper**

Village National Historic District. A catalog of the buildings is available at the library, across from the Village Hall. A marker notes that the first white Irish potato in America was planted in the adjacent "Common Field."

North of Derry, the ◆ **Chester Village Cemetery** dates from 1751 and contains monuments by a number of master colonial stonecarvers. Look especially at the faces of the angels, a common motif on tombstones of the period. The story is that stoneworker Abel Webster, who lived in Chester in the 1700s, had a running theological quarrel with the townspeople, and to get even with them he put frowns on the faces of all the angels on the tombstones. At the crossroads of Routes 121 and 102 in Chester.

AMOSKEAG

Scouts and leaders will want to stop on the way into Manchester at one of the finest collections of Boy Scout memorabilia and books in the United States. The ◆ **Lawrence L. Lee Scouting Museum** is located at the headquarters of the Daniel Webster Council, where there are also picnic tables and camping facilities. Covering more than 3,000 feet of floorspace, the museum houses more than 95 percent of all Scout books written in the United States, as well as historic uniforms, worldwide postage stamps commemorating scouting, and the original paintings used for covers of *Boy's Life*. Open 10:00 A.M. to 4:00 P.M. daily in July and August, weekends only in September through June, on Bodwell Road in Manchester; call (603) 669–8919 for more information.

Although it's hard to miss the red-brick factory buildings that run the length of Manchester, you should visit the ◆ **Manchester Historical Association** for a closer look at how these mills shaped the past and present of this manufacturing city. On the main floor of the museum is an area for changing exhibits, which focus on a particular aspect of life or a period of history. These high-quality special exhibits give the curatorial staff a chance to look more closely at the subject and interpret the museum's many artifacts and documents. The museum encourages visitors to value their own collections, mementos, and family stories. Along with more recent history, the museum has a display of the earliest Indian relics found in New Hampshire, dating from the paleolithic era. Walking tours of historic neighborhoods and the mill complexes are offered in the summer and fall, by reservation for a $5.00 fee. The museum will tell you a lot about this hard-working city's blue-collar, down-to-earth history. There is a tiny gift shop on the first floor. The museum is free and nobody bothers you as you browse about, but your contribution will be appreciated even if there is no one to see you put it in the box. Open Tuesday through Friday 9:00 A.M. to 4:00 P.M. and Saturday, 10:00 A.M. to 4:00 P.M. You'll find it at 129 Amherst Street, Manchester; call (603) 622–7531.

For a no-frills meal, walk a couple of blocks to the **Red Arrow Lunch.** It will be open, whatever the time of day; it has been since 1903. The menu includes stuffed cabbage, chicken pot pie, liver and onions, and meat loaf—you get the idea. Most entrées are priced under $5.00. Breakfasts are as generous as dinner and just as inexpensive. Open twenty-four hours, seven days a week, all year, at 61 Lowell Avenue (between Chestnut and Elm streets) in Manchester (603–624–2221).

Manchester has a lot of little places to eat, many of them ethnic restaurants run by people who came from the country whose cuisine is featured. **The Athens,** on Central Street (603–623–9317), is good for hearty portions of Greek food. One of the newest additions to the state's expanding Asian repertoire is **Hyung Jea,** on the corner of Chestnut and Manchester streets. Authentic Korean dishes are served in pleasantly simple surroundings. The menu describes the contents if patrons need help unraveling the mysteries of unfamiliar names. The Daeji Bul Go Ki, spiced grilled pork with crisp-cooked onions, is a good choice for those who like moderately spicy foods. Close to the Palace Theater, Hyung Jea is a convenient spot for an early dinner before a performance. They do not take credit cards and they are closed on Sunday.

The French-Canadian influence is still strong here, with a daily French-language newspaper and the Association Canado-Americaine at 52 Concord Street (603–625–8577), whose library of more than 4,000 volumes centers on the development of French culture in North America. The west side of town, across the river, was the French-Canadian neighborhood, dominated by the impressive **Sainte Marie's Church.** The architecture is distinctive, and the stone interior is reminiscent of the cathedrals of Quebec and Montreal.

The ◆ **Currier Gallery of Art** displays permanent collections of American and European fine and decorative arts, as well as changing special exhibits and programs. Tours of the **Zimmerman House,** designed by Frank Lloyd Wright, begin here. The museum is open daily, except Tuesday, 11:00 A.M. to 5:00 P.M. and remains open until 9:00 P.M. on Friday. Admission is free Fridays from 1:00 until 9:00 P.M. The gallery is located at 192 Orange Street; telephone (603) 669–6144 for more information.

Behind the Manchester Historical Association, on Hanover Street between Chestnut and Pine streets, is a nicely designed and executed **wall mural** depicting the mill heritage that built Manchester. Continue up Hanover Street, away from the center of the city, to see some excellent examples of Victorian architecture lining both sides of the street.

The Merrimack River, whose power once operated machinery of the Amoskeag Mills, now produces electricity at the Amoskeag Hydro Station. When salmon were restored to the river a "fish ladder" was built to permit the fish to return to their spawning grounds. The Merrimack River Basin can support an adult salmon population of about 3,000, and visitors to the ◆ **Amoskeag Fishway** can watch the fish make their way up a series of stepped pools in late May. Large viewing windows allow visitors to observe fish at eye level. The fishway is open from late April until June with displays, programs, and films that illuminate the history, ecology, and wildlife of the river and of Manchester. Admission is free and the area is handicapped accessible. Enter from Fletcher Street, behind the TravelLodge at the Amoskeag Bridge; for exact opening times contact Public Service Company of New Hampshire, P.O. Box 330, Manchester 03105 or call them at (603) 626–FISH.

While hotels are plentiful in the city, B&B accommodation is rare. Travelers who prefer the surroundings of a finely kept home should call **Derryfield Bed & Breakfast.** Located in a quiet residential neighborhood with quick access to Interstate 93, Derryfield has surprisingly low rates. Breakfast is served overlooking the pool and surrounding woods, on a table set with fine china and crystal. Rooms must be reserved in advance at this small and very personal hostelry. The owner will meet guests at the airport, an unusual

27

and welcome service. The B&B is at 1081 Bridge Street Extension, Manchester 03104; telephone (603) 627–2082 for reservations.

A few miles west of Manchester in the village of Bedford is the **Bedford Village Inn.** The historic farmhouse is now the restaurant, and the massive barn has been converted into twelve guest suites and two apartments. Luxury is the keynote of the inn: King-sized four-poster beds, full-sized desks, marble bathrooms, whirlpool baths, full-sized sitting rooms, and a mixture of antique and reproduction furniture give style and comfort to this small modern hotel in an old setting. It's a pleasant combination. It is among the more expensive lodgings that we list, but it also offers a lot for the money.

The original farmhouse has been left much as it was, made into small dining rooms. A large dining room has been added at the back, glass-enclosed to look out over the garden, arbor, and barn. The menu offers a wide selection of choices, each dish with an individual touch. Salmon is grilled on a cedar plank, pork tenderloin is glazed with maple and thyme, chicken and veal are blended with artichokes and Madeira. Entrées begin at $17. Open daily for lunch and dinner. Write the Bedford Village Inn, Old Bedford Road, Bedford 03102. You can call the inn at (603) 472–2602 and the restaurant at 472–2001.

The only ❖ **public archery ranges** in New Hampshire are at Bear Brook State Park, northeast of Manchester. Maintained by the Fish and Game Department, each consists of fifteen targets. An additional four-target practice range is wheelchair accessible. The park includes several ponds, two marshes, and a wildlife refuge and offers swimming, tent camping, and fishing as well. Hiking trails, many of which become cross-country trails in the winter, cover the area.

One of the very few **Civilian Conservation Corps (CCC) camps** left in the northeast is in Bear Brook Park. The buildings house a CCC Museum, a Snowmobile Museum, a Nature Center, and the Museum of Family Camping. All are open daily Memorial Day through Labor Day, and some weekends during spring and fall. Much of the park land itself was part of the CCC camp during the 1930s, and many of the picnic sites, hiking trails, recreation buildings, and roads you will enjoy on New Hampshire's public lands were built by the CCC. Write Bear Brook State Park, Allenstown 03275 or call (603) 485–9874.

THE CAPITAL

Although it is important as the center of government for the state, Concord is not a large city. (Incidentally, if you want to immediately label yourself as an outlander, pronounce Concord as you would the usual noun. In New England, it's pronounced "conquered.") Its manufacturing remained small, and it retains even now the appearance of a stately turn-of-the-century city, with its brick business blocks and government buildings of gray granite.

Blending into these buildings that surround the statehouse is the ◆ **New Hampshire Historical Society.** The sculpture above the columned granite façade is the work of Daniel Chester French, creator of the *Minuteman* statue in Concord, Massachusetts, and the seated Lincoln in Washington, D.C. The collections of the society on permanent display include outstanding examples of New Hampshire furniture and decorative arts. Special exhibits may feature any aspect of New Hampshire history—a term not limited here, as it is so often, to events of previous centuries. Displays may highlight the Shakers, baseball, textile arts, or the life and times of a citizen, famous or little known.

The focal point is an original **Concord Coach.** Splendid in decorative detail, these coaches were as strong and as well constructed as they were beautiful. They were, in fact, so perfect in their design that from the 1820s to the early 1900s, during which time more than 3,000 of them were built in Concord, almost no changes were made in their construction. It was the most perfect traveling vehicle known to its times. Wells, Fargo and Company used them, and they have often been called "the coach that won the West."

The small museum shop in the historical society is an excellent source of publications on New Hampshire and its history. Many of these are privately printed and hard to find elsewhere. Open Monday to Friday, 9:00 A.M. to 4:30 P.M. and Saturday and Sunday, noon to 4:30 P.M. The New Hampshire Historical Society is at 30 Park Street in Concord; call (603) 225–3381.

Just north of Concord's downtown area, the ◆ **Kimball-Jenkins Estate** is the epitome of Victorian style and architecture. Eleven-foot ceilings, hand-carved oak woodwork, and the air of a well-run turn-of-the-century household characterize this home, which stands today exactly as it looked when it was the home of the Kimball family. The grounds that surround it are landscaped in period gardens. Visitors are taken on tours from June 1 until October 31, Tuesday through Sunday, 11:00 A.M. to 4:00 P.M. While appointments are not required, they are appreciated. The Kimball-Jenkins Estate is at 266 North Main Street in Concord; call (603) 225–3932.

Concord's arts calendar is enriched by the **Concord Community Music School,** which brings recitals, lunch-hour concerts, children's programs, and a variety of other classical and jazz performances to the area. For a complete schedule, write to the school at 23 Wall Street, Concord 03301 or call (603) 226–3151.

For lunches to eat in or take out in Concord, try the combo sandwiches and fine coffees at **Caffenio** at 84 North Main Street (603–229–0020) or the Pasta House, under Vercelli's on Depot Street.

There's no questioning the source of **Vercelli's** pasta: Guests can watch it being made as they enter the restaurant. In the Pasta Kitchen, separated from the foyer by a large window, fettucini, linguine, manicotti, tortellini, and other pasta varieties are made fresh each day. The menu, from antipasti to canoli, is enticing, with a wide selection of out-of-the-ordinary seafood dishes, such as a delectable combination of mozzarella, grilled shrimp, and fresh tomato with olive oil and lemon. Some of the most outstanding features of Vercelli's menu are the nine veal dishes offered, ranging from Involtini to Scaloppini Marsala, each meticulously prepared. Vercelli's is at 12 Depot Street; telephone (603) 228–3313.

At the north end of Concord is the ◆**Silk Farm Wildlife Sanctuary** and the headquarters of the New Hampshire Audubon Society. Trails traverse the forests and wetlands along the edge of Great Turkey Pond and cross orchards, hedgerows, and fields where visitors can see rare wildflowers as well as birds and small animals. Audubon House provides a year-round bird blind, an excellent wildlife library, and a shop featuring a variety of nature guides and gifts with a wildlife theme. It is open Monday through Saturday, 9:00 A.M. to 5:00 P.M., and Sunday, 1:00 to 5:00 P.M. The library is open Thursday and Saturday, 10:00 A.M. to 4:00 P.M. The New Hampshire Audubon Society is at 3 Silk Farm Road (off Clinton Street) in Concord, easily reached from Exit 2 off Interstate 89. Call (603) 224–9909 for more information.

Silk Farm Road leads into the back entrance of ✦ **St. Paul's School,** whose chapel has a finely executed fresco in the oratory to the left of its entrance, a replica of Lorenzetti's great fresco at Assisi. Two mobiles by Alexander Calder are also on the campus; one is suspended from the ceiling in the lobby of Memorial Hall, and the other is on the grounds nearby. The outdoor mobile is stored from November through March to protect it from the harsh winter weather.

A small, but very attractive, bed and breakfast nearby offers moderately priced rooms with private bath. Breakfasts are served overlooking the well-tended grounds of an avid gardener. Within a short walk, between School and Franklin streets, is a neighborhood filled with fine **Victorian houses,** many of which are carefully restored. The bed and breakfast is not in a restored historic home, but its comfort and hospitality are timeless. Write Charles and Harriet Ward, 43 North Fruit Street, Concord 03301 or call (603) 224–2620.

Across the river to the east, in Concord Heights, the Society for the Protection of New Hampshire Forests' ✦ **Conservation Center** maintains several buildings powered by alternative energy sources, as well as nature trails. This organization is responsible for the preservation of huge tracts of land throughout the state by either outright ownership, purchase of development rights, or helping private and governmental bodies in their efforts to save important lands and forests. You can tour their passive-solar building Monday through Friday, 9:00 a.m to 5:00 P.M., free of charge. There is also a gift shop featuring environmental gifts and publications. Take East Side Drive (Route 132) north from Bridge Street (Route 9) to a left turn onto Portsmouth Street (you will pass the other end of this street going to the right shortly before the turn you want). The address is 54 Portsmouth Street (603–224–9945).

SHAKER COUNTRY

East Side Drive becomes Mountain Road, still Route 132, which leads to Canterbury and the beautifully maintained ✦ **Shaker Village.** Set on a hill among rolling meadows, this was once a thriving 4,000-acre farm where 300 Shakers lived and worshiped in an atmosphere of common ownership, celibacy, and a strong

31

work ethic. In the twenty-two buildings of the village you will see original examples of Shaker crafts in the furnishings of the houses. Skilled craftspeople are at work with wood, fiber, and plants creating baskets, boxes, brooms, and herbal crafts. Authentic lunches and dinners are recreated in the Creamery, where they use herbs from the village's garden. Guided tours begin on the hour and take about ninety minutes. A gift shop features Shaker reproductions and New Hampshire crafts. Thomas Merton once observed, "The peculiar grace of a Shaker chair is due to the fact that it was built by someone capable of believing that an angel might come and sit on it." Both that grace and its spiritual origins are evident throughout the village. Open May through December, 10:00 A.M. to 5:00 P.M., weekends April, November, and December. Admission is $8.00 for adults and $4.00 for children ages six to sixteen. Write Canterbury Shaker Village, 288 Shaker Road, Canterbury 03224 or call (603) 783–9511.

The town of Tilton is inextricably linked with the Tilton family, who were the generous benefactors of much of the town's artistic heritage. Charles Tilton, like many cultured men of his times, believed in the importance of public statuary and began to set about ornamenting his home town. Overlooking the town from a steep hillside on the opposite side of the river is the ◆ **Tilton Arch,** an exact replica of the Arch of Titus in Rome. Built of Concord granite, it rises 55 feet from its base, upon which lies a red granite lion. It is actually in the town of Northfield, and you can get there via the bridge at the monument on Main Street, turning left on the far side, and going uphill to the Northfield Town Hall. Beside it, a dirt road leads to the top of the hill and the monument.

Five of Charles Tilton's statues remain. A marble allegorical statue of America—depicted as an Indian princess—stands on Main Street, as do statues symbolizing Europe and Asia. A zinc statue of Chief Squamtum now stands in a parking lot. An iron footbridge connects the town with an island, once the site of the Tilton summer house and now a shaded park.

Fine mansions still grace Tilton, and one of them, on West Main Street, is of particular interest. **The Black Swan** bed and breakfast is a beautiful preserved Victorian, filled with period architectural and decorative detail. One guest room includes a huge semicircular sitting room alcove with stained-glass panels over each of its seven windows. Each room has some distinctive

Tilton Arch

antique feature or furnishing, and the dining room is fully paneled in oak with built-in china cupboards and a fireplace. The gardens and lawns sweep down to the river banks, overhung by shade trees. It's a thoroughly enjoyable resting place at moderate prices. Write The Black Swan at 308 West Main Street, Tilton 03276; call (603) 286–4524.

Just up the street at 321 West Main Street, **Le Chalet Rouge** serves memorable French cuisine to a maximum of twenty guests. The menu changes frequently but always includes a selection of classic entrées such as trout amandine, steak au poivre, lamb with rosemary, or roast duck. It's in the high-moderate range. Open Tuesday through Saturday from 6:00 P.M.; not all credit cards are accepted. Since seating is limited, you should make reservations (603–286–4035).

A number of fine craftspeople have studios in or near Tilton. The **Country Braid House** is both workshop and showroom for hand-braided wool rugs. Visitors are welcome to tour the workshop and learn about rug braiding. Those who would like to try their hand at it will find rug braiding kits for sale. Open Monday through Saturday, 9:00 a.m to 4:00 P.M., on Clark Road in Tilton 03276 (603–286–4511).

CONTOOCOOK VALLEY

West of Concord lies an area of rolling farmlands and attractive villages. Hopkinton's wide Main Street is lined with trees and a number of homes of the colonial era. In the center of town on Main Street, the **New Hampshire Antiquarian Society** features a museum of early items. Open Monday, 1:00 to 5:00 P.M. and 6:30 to 8:30 P.M., and Wednesday, 9:00 to 11:00 A.M. and 1:00 to 5:00 P.M. Telephone (603–746–3825).

To see herbs and perennial flowers in an impressive garden setting, visit the ❖**Fragrance Shop,** where you'll find 253 varieties of field-grown plants for sale. A walk in their gardens is pure joy, and the eighteenth-century barn is filled with wreaths, herb crafts, dried flowers, potpourri, and culinary herb blends as well as garden accessories, such as sundials and bee skeps. Open mid-April through December, Tuesday through Saturday, 10:00 A.M. to 5:00 P.M., on College Hill Road in Hopkinton (603–746–4431).

◆**St. Andrew's Episcopal Church,** in the village center, has particularly fine stained glass windows and, unlike most churches, has a thorough printed history of them, researched and written by retired St. Paul's teacher, John Archer. The latest of these windows to be added is by Tiffany, a cross-and-lilies design much simpler than most Tiffany windows. You can get a copy of Archer's book and a key to the church from the office on weekdays. **Windyledge Bed and Breakfast** offers antiques-furnished guestrooms with a view of the mountains, in a hilltop colonial home. Breakfast may include a sour cream soufflé or apricot-glazed French toast. It is located on Hatfield Road, Hopkinton 03229; telephone (603) 746–4054.

The only Henniker on earth was named for a London merchant who was a friend of Royal Governor Benning Wentworth. New England College is in the center of town and gives it a lively air and a series of cross-country ski trails named for Marx Brothers movies. The toughest, which goes over a small mountain, is called "You Bet Your Life."

Skiing is not a new pastime in Henniker. For more than thirty years, the Patnaude family has operated one of New Hampshire's southernmost ski areas, ◆**Pats Peak.** The mountain doesn't have the altitude of the White Mountains ski areas, but it has nineteen trails that are well groomed and well divided among the different skill levels; 90 percent snowmaking coverage extends the season. The food in the base lodge is homemade, and it's the kind of family ski area where you don't mind your kids skiing alone. Ski school, nursery, rentals, and other facilities are offered, and ticket sales are limited to the number of people that the lifts can comfortably handle without overcrowding. Write Pats Peak, Route 114, Henniker 03242 or call (603) 428–3245 or (800) 742–7287.

In town, **Coffees** serves a tempting variety of brewed coffees in its cafe, along with baked goods and lunches. It is tucked away on a little side street, only a block from the center of the village, at 15 Rush Street; (603) 428–3929.

Fine dining and lodging are only a bit out of town at the **Colby Hill Inn,** a rambling New England hostelry that has been updated and renovated without losing its country inn flavor. The sixteen guest rooms, each with a private bath, and two with working fireplaces, are decorated with antiques. Details of decor and hospitality are all here—elegant bed linens, a full cookie jar, plenty of public rooms, and spontaneous and gregarious hosts. The location is perfect, surrounded by meadows and a backyard where you can watch pheasants as you sit in the perennial garden. In the winter, part of the backyard becomes a skating rink for guests. This is a full-service inn, so its prices are higher than those of a typical bed and breakfast, beginning at $85.00 for a double, including a full country breakfast.

The dining room at Colby Hill Inn serves dinner to the public as well as to inn guests—and a fine dinner, too, with a frequently changing menu. Chicken breast stuffed with lobster is their signature dish. The salmon is grilled to perfection, the veal Marsala tender, and the pork loin flamed in applejack and Amaretto. Service is very personal, but neither stifling nor too folksy—and the view from the dining room of the floodlit barn and carriage shed and clumps of white birches is lovely even in the drab gray of a snowless November evening. Dinner prices are in the upper-moderate range, with most entrées $15.00 to $20.00. The dining room is open year-round, Wednesday through Saturday, 5:30 to 8:30 P.M. and Sunday 4:30 to 7:30 P.M. Write Colby Hill Inn, The Oaks, Henniker 03242 or call (603) 428–3281.

The entire Contoocook valley abounds with antiques shops, and the Studio Fiber features hand-dyed yarns, beads, and supplies for spinning, weaving, and knitting as well as hand-woven fabrics and sheep-related gifts. It's at 9 Foster Hill Road off Routes 202 and 9 in Henniker (603–428–7830).

The Souhegan Valley

Zahn's Alpine Guest House, on Route 13, will bring back immediate fond memories to anyone who has traveled in Bavaria, Austria, or Switzerland. It looks and feels exactly like those warm, hospitable mountain chalets that welcome travelers throughout the Alps. A big tile stove fills one corner of the Stube, which doubles as breakfast room and guest lounge. The pine post-and-beam construction with deeply overhung roof provides each of the guest rooms with a sheltered balcony—rimmed with window boxes of bright flowers in the summer. Alpine antiques, multicolored rag rugs, big feather pillows, and wrought iron fixtures complete the scene, but Zahn's has not fallen prey to the temptation to make it "Ye olde Alpine cute." It's the real thing, as is the hospitality; rates are below our moderate range. In the winter, kids can go for dogsled rides at the adjacent Christmas Tree Farm while parents cut their own tree. To reserve a room, write to Zahn's at P.O. Box 75, Milford 03055; call (603) 673–2334 or fax (603) 673–8415.

The owners of Zahn's have been asked so often for directions to area antiques shops that they've printed a little map for their guests showing twenty-two different shops.

Also on Route 13, just as it leaves the center of Milford, is the **Colonel Shepard House.** Its white paneled dining rooms with lace curtains and swags provide a formal but relaxing setting for a fine meal. Along with a varied regular menu, the chef offers several innovative specials, such as venison in Zinfandel sauce. Particularly memorable is Chicken St. Jacques, a breast filled with tender scallops, each cooked to exactly the right point. The frog legs appetizer is enough for a main dish. Entrées range from $8.00 to $19.00. Open for dinner only, Tuesday through Sunday, 5:00 to 9:00 P.M. at 29 Mont Vernon Street, Milford 03055; telephone (603) 672–2527. The Colonel Shepard also has antiques-furnished guest rooms upstairs.

A refreshing change from most small museums that are open only in the summer, ❖**Beaver Brook Farm and Transportation Museum** in Mont Vernon, just north of Zahn's, is open Friday, Saturday, and Sunday, from Thanksgiving through New Year's Day, coinciding with the season of their adjacent Christmas Tree Farm. A narrow-gauge railroad, a fire engine display, a grist mill, Franklin Roosevelt's car, a Concord Coach, and a variety of sleighs, wagons, and buggies highlight the collections. Visits can be arranged at other times of year by advance reservation, but the museum is not open to casual drop-ins; there is no admission charge. Write to the museum at 78 Brook Road, Mont Vernon 03057, including your telephone number.

Water power was central to New Hampshire industry from the earliest days, and ❖**Frye's Measure Mill** is still operated by an upright turbine driven by water from two ponds. Actively engaged in the making of fine round and oval wooden boxes, just as the first ones were made here in 1858, the mill also operates 1½-hour tours on Saturdays from June through October. The mill shop sells the boxes made here as well as other early crafts.

Open April through December, from 10:00 A.M. to 5:00 P.M. The mill is on Davisville Road and Burton Highway in Wilton; call (603) 654–6581 for more information.

Not far from Frye's, on a winding country road that briefly becomes the main street of Wilton Center, **Stepping Stones Bed & Breakfast** stands among lovely tended terraced gardens. The gardens seem to move inside with you as you enter the sunny, plant-filled breakfast room, which overlooks the terrace through a solid wall of windows. Down comforters, wicker furniture, and vintage pieced coverlets make this lodging memorable, as does breakfast, which may feature corn quiche, almond omelet, or stuffed French toast as its main course. Pets and children are welcome here, but smoking is not. Stepping Stones, Bennington Battle Trail, Wilton Center 03086; telephone (603) 654–9048.

Six-tenths of a mile from Stepping Stones (follow the road toward Frye's, turning right and right again), you come to a stream. Park just before the bridge and follow the old road on foot to a pond, beyond which there is a lovely **cascade** on the left.

The town of Wilton (not to be confused with the village of Wilton Center) lies just to the north of Route 101. The prominent brick mill building has been transformed into shops and a cheerful café-restaurant called **Cafe Pierrot.** The tall windows and white painted brick make the dining area light and spacious. Light meals, which can double as appetizers, but are plenty for lunch, include an herbed shrimp sauté served over linguini, a delicate lemon jasmine chicken, or Brie with fresh baked bread. Dinner entrees range from chicken Creole to trout amandine, priced from $6.00 to $11.00. They are closed Monday. Cafe Pierrot is on Old Wilton Road, Wilton 03086; telephone (603) 654–9411.

THE MONADNOCK REGION

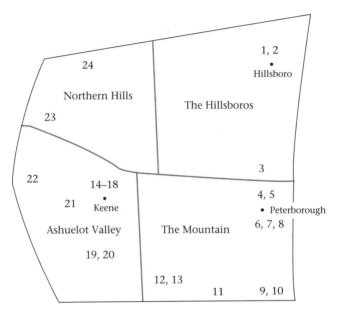

1. Hillsboro Center
2. Fox State Forest
3. Greenfield State Park
4. Peterborough Historical Society Museum
5. New England Marionette Opera
6. Temple Mountain Ski Area
7. Pack Monadnock Mountain
8. Birchwood Inn
9. Barrett House
10. Estelle M. Glavey Antiques
11. Cathedral of the Pines
12. Amos J. Blake House
13. Rhododendron State Park
14. Wyman Tavern
15. Barry Faulkner mural
16. Archive Center of the Historical Society of Cheshire County
17. Horatio Colony House Museum
18. Monadnock Children's Museum
19. Covered bridges
20. Swanzey Historical Museum
21. Chesterfield Gorge
22. Park Hill
23. Old Academy Museum
24. Bascom's Maple Farms

THE MONADNOCK REGION

Word has it that Mount Monadnock is no longer the second most climbed mountain in the world. With motorized access to Fujiyama's summit, fewer people are climbing it, so Monadnock may now be number one. Whichever, its rocky ledge summit on a fine summer day is definitely not off the beaten path. But its broad-shouldered cone standing alone with no other mountains for company is the focal point for an entire region. Views of it provide the backdrop for towns miles away, from Jaffrey, where most of the mountain lies, to Keene. On clear days it can be seen from as far away as Boston and the Green Mountains of Vermont.

Geologically, the mountain is the definitive *monadnock,* a mass of rock more durable, hence more resistant to erosion and glacial action, than the land around it. It is this mountain for which the geological phenomenon was named. The rest of the land of this southwest corner of New Hampshire is rolling, accented with small mountains and lakes. Only one city, Keene, is located in the entire area. It, and Peterborough, provide the cultural and business centers, but the smaller towns are surprisingly active, with their own museums, concert series, and theater groups. The bandstands that decorate the commons of Monadnock's towns are not there just to take pictures of. Painters, writers, and musicians have found a haven in this area for a century, giving it a rich tradition in the arts.

THE HILLSBOROS

Visitors from outside of New England often comment on the apparent lack of originality displayed in the naming of towns here. In one area will be found town after town with the same named prefixed by the four points of the compass or by *Center, Upper,* or *Lower,* or suffixed by *Falls, Mills, Junction, Street,* or *Depot.* The reason has to do with the town system of government, which was often based upon the original land grants. Large parcels of land were settled with several villages springing up within the boundaries of a town. Hillsboro is a good example. Within the limits of the town are Hillsboro, Hillsboro Center, Hillsboro Upper Village, and Hillsboro Lower Village.

❖**Hillsboro Center** is among New Hampshire's loveliest towns, its houses set around a circular road on a slight slope, with two churches. The entire center of the village is webbed with stone walls, testament to the number of rocks that northern New Englanders have had to pull out of their farmlands over the centuries. A well-preserved town pound, built to keep stray animals out of neighbors' gardens, completes this almost perfect village scene. Just outside of town, rows of nearly perfect double-stone fences border the fields of two exceptionally beautiful hillside farms.

◈**Fox State Forest** is a 1,448-acre area of managed forest that contains plantations of exotics (trees that do not grow here naturally) and some unusual protected natural areas as well. One of these is a black gum, or tupelo, swamp. This tree is common to the south but rarely found in New England. A ravine of mature hemlock and one of the state's rare stands of virgin forest are here, as well as a true sphagnum bog formed by a floating mat of moss filled with rare wild plants. More than 20 miles of hiking trails wind through the forest; cross-country skiers are welcome on the trails in the winter, but there are no other recreation facilities here, since this is a forest, not a park. You are welcome to picnic on the grounds (they have a few tables) as long as you respect the "carry-in, carry-out" policy. Open year-round from dawn to dusk. Look inside the mailbox by the entrance for a trail guide. Write Fox State Forest, Hillsboro Center Road, P.O. Box 1175, Hillsboro 03244 or call (603) 464–3453 for more information.

The boyhood **home of Franklin Pierce,** New Hampshire's only native son to become President of the United States, is just off Route 9 at the Lower Village. The mansion is a more elegant residence than was common in rural New Hampshire when it was built in 1804. Open Memorial Day to Columbus Day, Saturdays 10:00 A.M. to 4:00 P.M., Sundays 1:00 to 4:00 P.M., and Fridays in July and August, 10:00 A.M. to 4:00 P.M. It's on Route 31 at Route 9 in Hillsboro (603–478–3165).

As you go west on Route 9, look for an outstanding example of a double-stone arch bridge beside the road. It's worth a stop here to walk around to the upstream side for a better picture of what it looked like in the nineteenth century. You can go down under the present bridge to see the stonework of the old bridge as well as the river as it continues downstream through a mass of boulders.

◈**Greenfield State Park** reserves one sandy beach just for campers who have settled into its spacious, wooded tent sites and has another one for day visitors and picnickers. This is one of the rare places where you can rent a boat either for the fishing or to enjoy the quiet of Otter Lake. One of the smaller of New Hampshire's state parks and one of the least known, it is a perfect retreat for nature lovers, swimmers, and those who seek a place to paddle their canoe in peace. Write the park at P.O. Box 203, Greenfield 03047 or call (603) 547–3497.

The white-spired meeting house in **Hancock** is said to be the most-photographed church in the state, although it is hard to understand how such a statistic is determined. The entire town of Hancock invites photography with its neat rows of fine old buildings along the main street. **The Hancock Inn,** whose new owners have changed the inn's name as well as the decor, has been welcoming travelers for over two hundred years. One of its guest rooms has wall murals painted by the itinerant artist Rufus Porter; all rooms are furnished in a tasteful blend of antiques and newer pieces, with handmade quilts and queen size beds. In the dining room, which is open to the public, don't miss the Maine crabcakes, served with a light lemon sauce. Locally grown organic vegetables accompany the entrées. Write The Hancock Inn, Main Street, Hancock 03449 or call (603) 525–3318.

THE MOUNTAIN

Historical societies perform several valuable services to their towns, such as storing and preserving records of long-closed schools and businesses, providing a safe home for old photographs, maps, and books that would otherwise be lost, and offering a clearinghouse for historical and genealogical information. A few maintain museums based on purchases or gifts of local artifacts, furnishings, and property.

The ◆**Peterborough Historical Society Museum** is one of the finest historical museums of any society in the state. Along with exhibition rooms featuring early tools and antiques, they have in the several buildings of their complex a complete Victorian parlor, a replica of a country store, a colonial-era kitchen, and a restored mill house. Open year-round, Monday through Friday, 1:00 to 4:00 P.M. Tours available in July and August cost $1.00. The museum is at 19 Grove Street (P.O. Box 58), Peterborough 03458 (603–924–3235).

Peterborough has a theatrical heritage: Bette Davis began her career here at Mariarden, a theater summer school, in 1926, as a dancing fairy in *A Midsummer Night's Dream*. The town's newest theater is the ◆**New England Marionette Opera,** which stages full productions of operas such as *La Boheme* and *Madame Butterfly* in a 135-seat theater designed especially for the 32-inch actors. So real and captivating is the performance that the little figures are called back for curtain calls and stopped by applause following arias. Technique is so flawless that even those who don't care for opera enjoy the performances. The theater is on Main Street, Peterborough 03458; for reservations call (603) 924–4333.

The **Sheiling Forest** provides pleasant walking through fields and forests, following stone walls built by farmers of long ago trying to clear their fields of the oversupply of granite boulders with which New Hampshire was blessed. These are easy, level walks. On Saturdays there are programs for small woodlot owners on the care and management of woodlands. Open daily dawn to dusk year-round on Old Street Road in Peterborough.

Peterborough residents evidently have a taste for good food, since there are a number of culinary havens in town. The **Kernel Bakery** was making flaky croissants for Monadnock-region breakfast tables long before *croissant* became a household word. And they are half the price of inferior products elsewhere. Their doughnuts, Danish, cookies, Eccles cakes, and breads are just as good. You can get a cup of coffee here to go with your breakfast pastry, but alas, not a cup of tea. Closed Sunday, Monday, and middays. You'll find the Kernel Bakery on Jaffrey Road (Route 202) in Peterborough; call (603) 924–7930.

The **Peterborough Diner** on Depot Street is a really shiny silver diner—the kind with wedges of pie in a little glass case on the counter—and it opens at 6:00 A.M. every day of the week (603–924–6202). For quality take-out with an international flair, go to **Twelve Pine** in a little cottage on Summer Street. It's open Monday through Friday, 11:00 A.M. to 6:00 P.M., and Saturday, 11:00 A.M. to 3:00 P.M. (603–924–6140).

The menu at **Latacarta,** a small restaurant in a former theater, defies classification. Just as you assume from the gyoza dumplings, the teppanyaki beef, and the tempura that this is a Japanese menu, your eye catches the fettucini and shrimp or the

43

hummus, or the nachitos, enchiladas, Bavarian chicken, or fish and chips. Prices are moderate and the menu changes weekly. Open noon to 9:00 P.M. Tuesday through Saturday and noon until 7:00 P.M. on Sunday. A small adjoining café serves light dishes before and after dinner hours. Latacarta is at 6 School Street in Peterborough; call (603) 924–6878.

◆ **Temple Mountain Ski Area** is small, friendly, and a good place for kids to learn to ski. Instructors here seem to have a special knack for getting kids who are barely old enough to stand up on feet to be able to stand up on skis. Lifts are fast, and everybody here smiles. Ski rentals and special beginners' packages are available, and the chili in their slope-side lodge is hearty enough to keep you skiing until the lifts close, which is at 10:00 P.M. every evening. Night skiing is especially fun since you can watch the lights twinkle through the whole valley. Temple Mountain is on Route 101 in Peterborough; call (603) 924–6949.

Although not as well known as its sister mountain. ◆ **Pack Monadnock** in Miller State Park offers easy access to mountain-top views extending from Boston to the White Mountains and Vermont. A fee is charged for use of the auto road to the summit or you can climb it on foot by any of three hiking trails, each about 1½ miles long. Picnic areas and an observation tower are at the open summit. The entrance is on Route 101 opposite the Temple Mountain ski area.

The rambling ◆ **Birchwood Inn** is as much as part of the town of Temple as the neighboring white-spired church. Its low-ceilinged dining room is decorated with murals believed to be by Rufus Porter, an itinerant nineteenth-century painter. This family-run inn changes its dining room menu nightly, with a choice of three entrées. Lamb is the house specialty, prepared in a variety of ways; one of the other two dishes is always seafood. On Route 45, a few miles off of Route 101, in Temple, the inn is open year-round except April and serves dinner Tuesday through Saturday evenings from 6:00 until 9:00 P.M. (603-878-3285).

The ◆ **Barrett House** in New Ipswich, one of the state's most outstanding Federal mansions, remained in the Barrett family from its construction in 1800 until it was given to the Society for the Preservation of New England Antiquities in 1948. Ornamented with pilasters and a central pediment, it is said to have

44

been built as a wedding present to Charles Barrett, Jr., from his father. Furnished with the best that each generation of the family could afford, including imported china and even a glass harmonica, the house interprets the life of a wealthy New England textile manufacturer and farming family over the course of several generations. Teas with guest lecturers are held throughout the summer and special events such as a late May antiques show highlight their schedule. Open Thursday through Sunday, June 1 through October 15, with house tours hourly from 12 noon to 4:00 P.M. Admission is $4.00 with special rates for seniors and children. Take Route 124 to New Ipswich, then Route 123A. You can write them at Main Street, New Ipswich 03071, or telephone (603) 878–2517.

In the same town there is another house filled with antiques, but these are all for sale. ✦ **Estelle M. Glavey Antiques** fills an entire home, not with showrooms, but with fully furnished rooms of museum-quality antiques. This is no jumble of merchandise. Everything, from the oriental rug on the floor to the china on the table and the flame-stitched wing chair by the fire, is just as it would be in a home—but all for sale and clearly tagged with a price, not a code. The surprise is that the pieces are very reasonably priced, considering their quality and condition. Open all year daily except Monday on Route 124 (603–878–1200).

Windblown Ski Touring Center keeps 20 miles of trails well groomed for cross-country skiers. Along with their waxing shed and restaurant, the center offers a warming hut with "sleeping bag accommodations." The views are spectacular. It's on Route 124, 3 miles west of the town of New Ipswich; call (603) 878–2869 for more information.

✦ **Cathedral of the Pines** is an outdoor church as well as a national memorial to those who lost their lives in wartime military service. Services are held here by people of all faiths, using the various altars and wooded "chapels." The Memorial Tower holds a peal of Sheffield bells and a set of four Norman Rockwell bas-reliefs in memory of the women who served in the military. Even when Cathedral of the Pines is not open for services, you can walk through the grounds, a forest of tall pines atop a hillside, with views of Monadnock, Kearsarge, and southern Vermont. Off Routes 202 and 119 in Rindge; call (603) 899–3300 for more information.

Where other towns may be "postcard towns," Fitzwilliam is a "Christmas card town." Its white town hall and stately homes set around the snow-covered common make it a favorite for artists and photographers creating greeting cards. One of these buildings on the common is the ◆**Amos J. Blake House,** a museum maintained by the Fitzwilliam Historical Society. Built in 1837, this was the home and law office of a well-respected community leader. His law office is intact, and other rooms are furnished in period antiques. A kitchen, parlor, music room, and reconstructed schoolroom are part of the museum, as are displays of military and firefighting memorabilia. A small shop, filled with local crafts, New England food specialties, soaps, and gifts, uses original country-store counters, furnishings, and cash register. Admission is free. Open late May to mid-October, Saturday, 10:00 A.M. to 4:00 P.M., and Sunday, 1:00 to 4:00 P.M. Write the Blake House, On the Common (P.O. Box 87), Fitzwilliam 03447 or call (603) 585–6642.

One of the largest stands of wild rhododendrons north of the Allegheny mountains is in Fitzwilliam at ◆**Rhododendron State Park.** The fifteen acres of large shrubs bloom by mid-July in a riot of huge flower clusters against glossy, deep green leaves. At any time of year the trails through this park are bordered by masses of broad evergreen leaves and the thick tangle of trunks and branches that support them. An adjoining wildflower trail was created by the Fitzwilliam Garden Club. Native plants are labeled in the open woodland that borders the path. It is a lovely, quiet, and cool spot, with 1 mile of easy walking. Follow the signs off Route 119.

A back road that branches off Route 12, not far north of the rock ledges, gives more views of Monadnock as well as a stone bridge. It brings you to Route 124 and into Marlborough. At the intersection with Route 101 is the **Homestead Bookshop.** Strong in local history, they have several shelves of long-out-of-print books on New Hampshire as well as a travel section well stocked with the works of explorers and adventurers. In addition to finding nearly 50,000 used books, you will meet the nicest people there. Their book search service ferrets out books for customers in all parts of the country. Open Monday through Friday, 9:00 A.M. to 5:00 P.M., and Saturday and Sunday, 9:00 A.M. to 4:30 P.M. Call (603) 876–4213 for more information.

ASHUELOT VALLEY

Keene's main street is lined for several blocks by beautifully cared-for private residences covering all architectural periods since the mid-eighteenth century. In the 1750s, the founders of Keene laid out all of the main lots so that the buildings would be set well back from the center of the highway. That decision set the tone for the development of downtown. At the north end of Main Street stands a large white church with a wedding cake spire. This is one of the most beautiful of New England's churches, and its location at the head of Central Square gives it a commanding presence.

On the west side of Main Street is the ochre-colored eighteenth-century ◆**Wyman Tavern.** It was from this tavern that a contingent of Keene Minutemen departed to join in the Revolution on April 23, 1775, four days after the battle at Concord, Massachusetts. Prior to that, the first trustees' meeting of Dartmouth College was held here. The tavern is now a museum, furnished in the 1770–1820 period. It is open June 1 to Labor Day, Thursday through Saturday, 11:00 A.M. to 4:00 P.M., and the admission is $2.00. You'll find the Wyman Tavern at 339 Main Street in Keene (603–357–3855).

A short distance up the street from the tavern is Elliot Hall. The large brick building set back from the street is now part of Keene State College. In the spiral staircase of its front hall is a ◆**Barry Faulkner mural,** depicting Central Square in Keene. Keene has several other examples of the work of this noted muralist whose work adorns the National Archives and Capitol Building in Washington, D.C. The lobby of Fleet Bank beside the church at the head of Central Square is decorated with his *Men of Monadnock* series. The Cheshire Medical Center on Court Street displays three smaller mural panels moved from another building, and the Keene Public Library has sketches made for his murals located elsewhere.

Other Barry Faulkner works are on display across lower Main Street in the ◆**Archive Center of the Historical Society of Cheshire County.** Along with the Faulkner works, the museum's collections include a room dedicated to locally manufactured Hampshire pottery and examples of Keene and Stoddard glass. It is at 246 Main Street, Keene 03431 and is open Monday through Friday from 9:00 A.M. to 4:00 P.M. Call (603) 352–1875.

One of the state's most unusual "old house" museums is in this same neighborhood, next to St. Bernard's Church on Main

Wyman Tavern

Street. The ◆ **Horatio Colony House Museum** is not a home restored to one particular period, but the residence of a twentieth-century heir to a fortune that allowed him to live the life of a nineteenth-century gentleman of leisure. He traveled all over the world, collecting as he went, with a fine eye and highly cultured tastes. The oriental art he brought back with him is at home in the 1806 Federal mansion amid the fine eighteenth- and nineteenth-century furnishings. Some of his collections are in glass cases in the ell, while other items are displayed as he lived with them. You will leave feeling that you have known this well-read, well-traveled, and generous gentleman who left his estate for others to enjoy. Open mid-May to mid-October, Tuesday through Saturday,

11:00 A.M. to 4:00 P.M., and Saturdays year-round. Admission is free; park behind the church. The address is 199 Main Street in Keene; call (603) 352–0460.

Across the street is **176 Main,** a casual restaurant serving a wide selection of soups, sandwiches, and entrées. The calamari appetizer is large enough to serve as a main course, and sandwiches are imaginative, perfect with a pint of one of their hard-to-find beers. 176 likes to encourage micro-brewerys so the list changes frequently. A terrace makes this casual restaurant particularly appealing during warm weather. At 176 Main Street, Keene 03431; telephone (603) 357–3100.

You don't have to be a child to enjoy the ✦**Monadnock Children's Museum.** Its upbeat, lively atmosphere and timely, colorful exhibits invite touching, exploring, and getting involved. Exhibits change, but you're sure to find fish, bubbles, musical instruments (ever heard a fanny fiddle?), a design-making pendulum, a light table, mineral exhibits, puppets, and a train set. A full schedule of activities, workshops, field trips, craft lessons, musical events, and interactive programs adds to the general air of busy-ness and excitement. In the front yard are a playhouse and wooden boat that kids just can't stay out of. The world room changes times and places as it explores cultures such as that of Tibet, medieval France and the French heritage, or the Abenaki. Open 10:00 A.M. to 4:00 P.M. every day except holidays; admission is $2.50 no matter how old or young you are. It's a good investment for adults—you'll feel years younger when you leave. The museum is at 147 Washington Street in Keene (603–357–5161).

Keene's favorite place for a quick breakfast or lunch is **Timoleon's,** on Main Street, just south of Central Square. This is the sort of place where everyone calls the waitresses by their first names, and the menu has all of the old favorites. They are noted for chicken croquettes, meat loaf, and on Friday, codfish cakes. At 25–27 Main Street, Keene 03431; telephone (603) 357–4230.

The **Fine Arts Center at Keene State College** has an active performance schedule (603–357–4041) and Keene supports its own choral group, the Keene Chorale. Their professional-quality concerts are held in the spring and before Christmas and may include sacred works such as masses and oratorios or operatic choral selections. For a schedule of concerts call (603) 357–1534. During the summer, concerts featuring popular bands are held on

Wednesday evenings at the bandstand in the common on Central Square from 7:00 to 8:30 P.M. (603–357–9829).

Swanzey, directly south of Keene, has maintained and preserved three ◆**covered bridges** over the Ashuelot River. The following route will show you all of them. Leave Keene on Route 10 (Winchester Street) and turn left on Matthews Road just past the veterinary clinic. Go left at the end and through the first of the bridges. When that road ends, go left again and shortly join Route 32 at the Potash Bowl (remember where this is—we'll get back to it later). All this sounds complicated, but it's a distance of only 3 to 4 miles. Go south on Route 32 to Carleton Road, where you will find another bridge in a few hundred yards. If it's early spring and the water is high, the bridge may be closed, but you can drive down to watch the river lapping at its floorboards. Return to Route 32 and continue south to Swanzey Lake Road on your right. Follow this winding road until it ends at a T. Go right, and you'll come to West Swanzey. The third bridge is to your left when you reach the crossroads at the top of the hill. Go through it, then turn right, and you will come to Route 10, which leads back to Keene (turn right).

Covered bridges did not originate in New England—they were a common sight in the Alpine regions of Europe for the same reasons early New Englanders built them. The roof protected floorboards and support timbers from the harsh weather and snow buildup that would weaken or break the bridge under its weight. Snow falling on the sloping roof would slide off, as it does on a house roof. The biggest job for road agents was shoveling snow *onto* the bridge so that sleigh runners could slide over them in the time of year when the sleighs replaced carriages and wagons for transport. (In New England, the term "road agent" means the person whose job it is to maintain roads. It does not refer to a highwayman, as it does in many other places.)

If you go left at Route 10 instead of right, you'll come to the ◆**Swanzey Historical Museum** on your left, a newly opened building with some unusually interesting exhibits. Here you will find an operational Amoskeag steam fire pumper made in Manchester and a stagecoach. The museum is wheelchair accessible and is open June through October, Monday to Friday, 1:00 to 5:00 P.M., and Saturdays and Sundays, 10:00 A.M. to 6:00 P.M. on Route 12 in Swanzey; call (603) 352–4579 for more information.

Carleton Bridge

For more than fifty years, the town of Swanzey has performed Denman Thompson's *The Old Homestead* at an open-air natural arena known as the **Potash Bowl.** Thompson's down-home plays, filled with moral lessons and country values, delighted New York theater audiences of the Victorian era. This play, performed each July, is a real period piece. Bring lawn chairs or blankets to sit on. Admission is $5.00 (603–352–0697).

◆**Chesterfield Gorge** shows the power of persistence. A relatively small brook has worn a deep gorge through the rocks here as it cascades from pool to pool for a distance of about ¼ mile. It is an easy hike, just over ½ mile, through a forest of beech and hemlock of unusual size. A small pavilion at the head of the trail contains information on the geologic history of the gorge's formation. A shady grove provides a good place for a picnic. The gorge is on Route 9, west of Keene.

Farther west, Route 63 crosses, leading south to Chesterfield and the entrance to ◆**Pisgah** (pronounced "Piz-gee") **State Park.** The road to this wilderness preserve winds along the edge of a hill through mixed hardwood forests. There are no facilities in the 13,000 acres of this park, and camping is not allowed. Hiking and ski trails crisscross the area, which is a favorite with fishermen and hunters. Some of the trails connect with **Road's End Farm Horsemanship Camp,** on Jackson Hill Road, and you're welcome to hike these trails as well. For ten weeks in the summer the camp is filled with girls sharing the experience of riding and caring for the camp's horses. In other seasons, experienced riders can call for reservations to enjoy these same trails and the views of Pisgah Park, Mount Monadnock, and even Mount Snow in Vermont. The farm's hilltop setting is unparalleled, and its gregarious owners hope to share it in the future by offering B&B accommodations. But for now, it's just for riders. Jackson Hill Road, Chesterfield 03443. Call (603) 363–4900.

If you follow it northward, Route 63 winds along the shore of Spofford Lake and into Westmoreland (pronounced with the accent on "west") and on through the settlement of ◆**Park Hill,** a cluster of noteworthy early buildings, the likes of which are rare outside of Portsmouth or Exeter. The Meeting House is one of the state's earliest, built in 1762 with a façade and spire considered among the finest in their period of architectural design and detail. The Paul Revere bell was placed there in 1827.

Around the church are several early homes, dating from as early as 1774.

Route 63 winds past some of New Hampshire's finest and most fertile farmland, with meadows full of grazing cattle and views across the Connecticut River valley into Vermont. From mid-February until mid-April and from mid-September until the end of November you can stop for breakfast, lunch, or a snack at **Stuart and John's Sugar House.** It's best in late February and into March when the sap is running and the back room is filled with steam from the evaporators. The corn fritters and homemade doughnuts are delicious, and syrup comes in a full-sized milk pitcher that the waitress plunks on the table when she brings the menu. All you need to decide is what to pour it over. If it's not breakfast or lunch time when you are passing by, try a maple sundae, frappé, or, in the fall, maple apple pie. This place isn't fancy; you sit on folding chairs at church supper-style tables. It's family style, family run, and a favorite low-cost Sunday outing for local families. Open weekends only, until 3:00 P.M. on Route 63 at Route 12 in Westmoreland (603–399–4486).

NORTHERN HILLS

Walpole looks down onto Route 12, and this picture-perfect village is a good place to stroll and admire the beautifully preserved and maintained eighteenth- and nineteenth-century homes that encircle the green. On Sunday evenings during July and August, band concerts fill this grassy common with music and people.

The prosperity that built the many homes and public buildings in Walpole resulted from the building of a canal around the Great Falls of the Connecticut River in 1790, which allowed river traffic (water was the main means of moving goods in those days) to proceed past here to the north country. The heirlooms of many of these early families have found their way to the ◆**Old Academy Museum.** Silk dresses with the kind of needlework that only prosperous women had the time to pursue have been preserved here along with furniture, tools, utensils, and kitchenware and a completely restored schoolroom from the original academy. Shaker furniture, and the original piano mentioned in *Little Women,* a gift to the Alcott sisters when they were living in Walpole, are just a few of the treasures that have been presented

53

Old Academy Museum

to the museum. Open from 2:00 to 4:00 P.M. Saturday and Sunday in July and August on Main Street in Walpole; call (603) 756–3449 for more information.

On Saturdays, stop at the Bellows House Bakery for cookies, French breads, muffins, and brownies. It is open from 8:00 A.M. to 2:00 P.M. Saturdays only, on North Main Street at High Street, Walpole (603–756–4250).

If you have a spare day and a sense of adventure, you could take any road out of Walpole and follow it until it ends in the dooryard of a farmhouse or bumps into Route 12A. The hillsides are covered with well-kept farms and are separated by lovely little hollows. The views over the valley are beautiful when you reach the hillcrests, most of which have been cleared for pasture land. North of Walpole, Route 123 heads into more hills, following the Cold River (*all* rivers here are cold; one wonders who decided that this one should be so honestly named). From the village of Drewsville, a road heads north toward Langdon, and in about a mile it passes New Hampshire's shortest covered bridge, only 36 feet long.

East of Alstead on Route 123A is another covered bridge and signs for ◆**Bascom's Maple Farms.** From mid-March through the first week in April, while the sap runs, Bascom's evaporators, both the ultramodern osmo-separators and the old-fashioned steaming pans, produce syrup that will be shipped all over the world. It's a warm steamy place to be on a windy March day, and after you've watched sap becoming syrup, you can sample the traditional New England treat, sugar on snow. Actually, it's syrup on snow, and it makes a chewy candy that is always served with a dill pickle to balance its sweetness. Doughboys with syrup, maple pecan pie, and maple milkshakes are available here, and you can eat them at long tables covered with red-checked oilcloth. Bascom's sells syrup, maple cream, and candies throughout the year and will ship gifts for you as well. Maple treats are served in March and early April (call to make sure the run has begun), Saturday and Sunday, 11:00 A.M. to 5:00 P.M. Write Bascom's at R.R. 1, Box 137, Alstead 03602 or call (603) 835–2230 or 835–6361. Syrup and candy are sold during regular business hours on weekdays year-round.

THE DARTMOUTH-SUNAPEE REGION

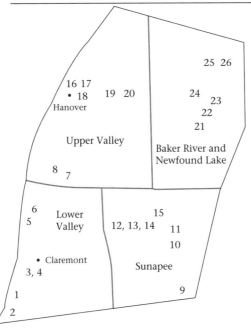

1. The Fort at No. 4
2. Main Street National Historic District
3. Claremont Village Industrial District
4. West Claremont
5. Northstar Canoe Livery
6. Saint-Gaudens National Historic Site
7. Covered railroad bridges
8. Pollard's Mills Falls
9. Mt. Kearsarge Indian Museum
10. Nunsuch Dairy
11. Andover Historical Society Museum
12. Philbrick-Cricenti Bog
13. Lake Sunapee
14. Sunapee Historical Museum
15. The Fells
16. Baker Memorial Library
17. Hood Museum of Art
18. The Hanover Inn
19. Lower Shaker Village
20. Canaan Street
21. Profile Falls
22. Wellington State Park
23. Paradise Point Nature Center
24. Sculptured Rocks
25. The Quincy Bog
26. Town Pound

THE DARTMOUTH-SUNAPEE REGION

The Connecticut River flows through a broad, flat valley as it forms the border between New Hampshire and neighboring Vermont. Along its shores and up the hillsides that overlook it are sprawling farmlands: fields of corn, herds of cattle, truck farms, and family farms. Their massive barns and tall, round silos punctuate the landscape. These venerable homes were built by some of the earliest settlers in the valley.

The farms were not always so serene. The river was the major artery of travel for the Indians as well as the settlers, and the French and Indian War was fought along its banks. It was to educate Indians that Eleazer Wheelock founded a school that is now Dartmouth College. Its cultural influence and that of Colby-Sawyer College in nearby New London on the entire upper valley are significant, especially in the performing and fine arts.

To the east of the Connecticut River valley rise the gentle slopes of Mounts Sunapee, Kearsarge, and Cardigan—each about 3,000 feet in altitude—and other smaller mountains. The Appalachian Trail crosses the river on its way south, and nearly every mountain in the region, however small, has a trail to its summit.

Lakes dot the landscape. This region is a quiet part of the state, and even the interstate that bisects it hasn't changed that. In fact, from the point where I–89 leaves Concord until it arrives in Lebanon, at the Vermont border, there is almost no commercial activity visible along its sides, only miles of forest and farmland backed by mountain vistas.

THE LOWER VALLEY

❖ **The Fort at No. 4** was once the northwesternmost English-speaking village in the New World. This museum is an authentic reconstruction of the settlement founded there in 1740. It is New England's only living history museum of the period of the French and Indian War. Within its log stockade are furnished province houses and shops where costumed interpreters carry on the daily work of an isolated colonial village. Dinner is prepared in a huge open fireplace, candles are hand dipped, and wool and flax spun and woven. From the lookout tower, sentries kept watch over the river and valley for signs of attack by the Indians or the

French. The skirmishes that took place here in those early years are re-created in full costume each year, and a cloud of smoke from musket fire hangs over the river as it did two-and-a-half centuries ago when, in 1747, it was besieged by a force of 400, but withstood the attack. This success resulted in the withdrawal of French forces to Canada and the beginning of English supremacy in northern New England. Of particular interest here is a working blacksmith shop, where a master smith creates the tools and utensils necessary for daily life and work on the frontier. A museum shop carries items of the period at extraordinarily reasonable prices. Open daily from Memorial Day through foliage season in October, from 10:00 A.M. to 4:00 P.M. every day except Tuesday. Admission is $6.00 for adults and $4.00 for children ages six to eleven. The Fort at No. 4 is on Route 11 (Box 336), Charlestown 03603; call (603) 826–5700.

Charlestown's ❖ **Main Street National Historic District** is lined with distinguished homes, many dating from the early 1800s. It is almost a mile long, and fifty-two of its sixty-three buildings are historically important; ten of them date from the 1700s. The Unitarian Church and two of the houses were designed by Stephen Hassam, great-grandfather of the impressionist painter Childe Hassam, who often painted the Isles of Shoals. St. Catherine's Church has four signed Tiffany stained-glass windows. Stop at the office of the town clerk for an inexpensive booklet describing the history of each building. One of the homes listed is **Maple Hedge B&B,** with antique-furnished guest rooms on Main Street, Charlestown 03603; telephone (603) 826–5237.

Claremont's early settlers quickly saw the potential of the waterfalls in the Sugar River as it flows from Lake Sunapee to the Connecticut River. The first dam was built in 1767 for a grist and saw mill, and other plants soon followed, their machinery powered by the force from the 300-foot drop in the river as it passes through town. Mill buildings still dominate the center of Claremont, and you can learn how they once operated by following a walking tour of ❖ **Claremont Village Industrial District.** A free brochure available from the Chamber of Commerce on Tremont Square describes the original uses and evolution of various buildings, including mill workers' housing, owners' residences, shops, the foundry, weave shed, and others, each of which is marked on an accompanying map.

59

The manufacturing that created the massive mills along the Sugar River also created the wealth to build Claremont's imposing new City Hall in 1897, with its tall, prominent clock tower. On its third floor it boasted an opera house with the largest stage north of Boston. Although the **Claremont Opera House and Atrium** now has a separate handicapped-accessible entry, those who enter through the old building can enjoy the carved archway and oak paneling of the lower lobbies and public areas. The large opera house has a curved balcony and cast-iron-based seats; open one to see its unique reclining back. This outstanding example of public architecture of the last century still hosts varied performances on a regular basis. It is open for performances and from 9:00 A.M. to 5:00 P.M. on weekdays. Call (603) 542–1296 for hours or (603) 542–4433 for a schedule of events.

If the Boccia sisters ever tire of running their fruit store and lunch counter across the street from Claremont's City Hall, they can simply turn it into a museum and charge admission. At the **George Boccia Fruit Store,** drinks still come out of the big red Coke coolers in the middle of the floor or the refrigerated glass-front wall chests. A substantial collection of Coca-Cola advertising decorates the upper walls. A deli counter displays the day's salads, quiches, and soups—if you can't decide between the chicken salad and the equally delicious Portuguese sausage-and-rice salad, ask for a plate with a sampling of each. It will come with a thick slice of Rondy's bread; her sister Maria makes the salads and their mother tends the cash register from behind an old glass display case. A few small tables fill the front of the store; you can eat there and listen to the good-natured banter between the Boccias and their customers. The shop is at 66 Tremont Square, Claremont 03743; telephone (603) 542–9816.

To the west, about 3 miles on Route 103, is the settlement of ◆ **West Claremont.** A road to the left leads across an old dam with mill foundations and again left to two historic churches. Union Church, a large, white clapboard building with curved windows, is the oldest Episcopal church building in New Hampshire. It is a surprise to see the oldest one this far inland—and this far from any present-day settlement. Its only neighbor, directly across the street, is St. Mary's Church, the first Roman Catholic church in the state, built between 1823 and 1825. The priest who established St. Mary's parish was the son of the Episcopal rector of

Union Church across the street. The son had converted to Catholicism. The two men conducted a school for the children of West Claremont mill workers in the second floor of St. Mary's. Today, these vanguard churches stand alone, surrounded only by West Part Burying Ground, the settlement they once served long gone.

The Connecticut River flows peacefully between its wooded shores, perfect for traveling by canoe. You can rent a canoe at ❖**Northstar Canoe Livery** in Cornish for half-day, full-day, or overnight trips on the Connecticut. The livery provides a shuttle that carries canoes and passengers upstream to put-ins either 4 or 12 miles distant. The 12-mile trip takes four to four-and-one-half hours; canoe rental and the shuttle are $17.00 per person. An overnight trip can be arranged so that you can camp on an island in the middle of the river. (You're still in New Hampshire, since New Hampshire owns to the normal high-water mark on the Vermont side. When it floods, Vermont owns the excess.) Northstar Canoe Livery is at Balloch's Crossing, Route 12A, in Cornish (603–542–5802).

The bridge across the Connecticut at Cornish is the **longest covered bridge in the United States.** (The longest in New Hampshire is at Bath; this one doesn't count since its other end is in Vermont.) Built in 1886, it traverses the river in two spans and has an unusual timber lattice-truss construction. At the turn of this century, Cornish was the home of a thriving colony of artists, writers, poets, and patrons who built or purchased summer homes around the studio of Augustus Saint-Gaudens. Italian terraced gardens surrounded old farmhouses, and the summer season's social life was one of wealthy bohemia.

The artists are gone, but the genius of the sculptor who attracted them to this retreat lives on in his beautifully situated home. His sculptures are displayed in the studios and galleries and throughout the grounds of the ❖**Saint-Gaudens National Historic Site.** The gardens and grounds, lined with tall pine and hemlock hedges and delicate birch trees, are worth a visit in their own right. The original Stanford White bluestone base for the statue of Admiral David Farragut has recently been moved here from New York City where it was being damaged by pollution. The house, just as Mrs. Saint-Gaudens left it, is filled with artworks, each piece with some personal significance. A spirited house tour brings the family to life and lifts this site above the usual "home of a famous person" category. Sunday afternoon concerts in the

Saint-Gaudens National Historic Site

summer bring musicians of all styles, along with music lovers carrying picnic baskets to the estate's shaded lawns. The house is open 8:30 A.M. to 4:30 P.M. daily from Memorial Day through late October; the grounds remain open until dusk. Admission is $2.00, free for ages under 16. Write to Saint-Gaudens National Historic Site, Box 73, Cornish 03745 or call (603) 675–2175.

Directly east of Claremont, Newport also preserves its late-nineteenth-century downtown. A busy rail line once connected these two towns, crossing the Sugar River twice on its way. The route is now a walking trail, level and smooth, covering 9.7 miles along the river. En route, it passes through two rare ◆ **covered railroad bridges,** the Chandler Station and Wrights. The former is clearly visible and both are accessible from Sugar River Drive, a dirt road that parallels the south bank of the river. From Claremont, take Broad Street (next to the park beside City Hall) to Chestnut and then left on Sugar River Drive. You can reach the path from Broad Street beyond the Chestnut Street intersection if you want to walk or bike the whole distance, or you can pick up the path at any of several points where it crosses Sugar River Drive.

A cool place to while away a hot summer afternoon is ◈ **Pollard's Mills Falls.** Actually a long series of small falls on the South Branch of the Sugar River, the cascades work their way through several hundred feet of a granite chasm lined with boulders. A path through the trees at the top of the embankment brings you to the site of the old mills, their rough stone foundations very evident along the shore of the stream. Be sure to find the large square hole cut into the bedrock to anchor the machinery of the mill. To get to the Falls, follow Route 11 west of Newport about ½ mile and take a left onto Unity Road. Follow this for about a mile and then take a left onto Pollard's Mills Road. About $\frac{4}{10}$ mile further, turn right at a Y in the road. Just around that corner is a parking area overlooking the falls. The path is to the left.

SUNAPEE

We have no intention of entering the historical dispute over the original meaning of *sunapee* in the Indian languages. It's a lovely region, in any language, with the mountain and lakes of the same name and the succession of smaller lakes between Mount Sunapee and Mount Kearsarge.

To the south lies Warner, with its ◈ **Mt. Kearsarge Indian Museum**.The museum's spirit is probably best summed up in the words of Chief Seattle in the late 1800s: "Every part of the earth is sacred to my people . . . every shining pine needle, every sandy shore, every light mist in the dark forest . . . we are part of the earth and it is part of us." The purpose of the museum is not so much to show the incomparable artifacts as to interpret the lifestyle through art and culture and to renew in all of us the positive relationship the Indians experienced between the earth and its people. It succeeds. The exhibits are the lifetime collection of Charles (Bud) and Nancy Thompson, who didn't want to have "a mausoleum of pickled artifacts," but rather a museum with a voice.

The voice is that of Indians. Except for the quotations, there are no written labels or signs in this beautifully displayed collection. Instead, a docent accompanies each visitor or group, explaining the displays focusing on those things that catch the visitor's interest. A museum shop sells authentic Indian handwork such as rugs, beadwork, and pottery, as well as books about various Indian tribes. Outdoors, a self-guided walk leads through two acres of native plants and trees used for medicine and food. Open May through October, Monday through Saturday, 10:00 A.M. to 5:00 P.M. and Sunday 12:00 noon to 5:00 P.M.; weekends, November to mid-December 12:00 noon to 5:00 P.M. Admission is $5.00 for adults and $3.00 for children ages six to twelve. Write Mt. Kearsarge Indian Museum, Kearsarge Mountain Road, P.O. Box 142, Warner 03278 (603–456–2600).

As you drive New Hampshire's roads you will see a number of domesticated animals from the expected cow to the exotic llama. ❖**Nunsuch Dairy** in South Sutton raises Taggenburg goats. A small dairy by commercial standards, Nunsuch produces rondelles of goat cheese that are sought by the area's top restaurants. You can stop to visit this meticulously clean dairy and meet the enthusiastic owner, Courtney Haase. Prices on the cheese are phenomenally low—an eight-ounce rondelle for $3.00. Pack a chunk of Nunsuch cheese for a lunch when you climb Mount Kearsarge, or take it on a picnic to a nearby shady roadside spot. Nunsuch Dairy is on Route 114, South Sutton 03221; call (603) 927–4176. (Courtney also sells gift packages of cheese on a goat-shaped board by mail: write Nunsuch Dairy, Star Route, Bradford 03221.)

In the Victorian-era railroad station at the village of Potter Place, the ❖**Andover Historical Society Museum** has interesting collections, including an original Western Union Telegraph office. The building itself is intact, a fine example of the ornamented stations that once lined the tracks throughout New England. One of the highlights of the museum is a dugout canoe that is in very good condition; outside on the tracks are a caboose and a plow car used to clear the tracks during snow storms. Open Saturday 10:00 A.M. to 3:00 P.M. and Sunday 1:00 to 3:00 P.M.

A short distance from Potter Place on Route 4 is the workshop of **The Village Whittler.** Wally Whitford specializes in deep relief carvings of local wildlife painted in colors so realistic that the trout appears to be jumping out of the wood panel. Loons are his most popular carving—you may have to wait for one of those, but he takes orders. Unique walking sticks begin at $5.00 in this tiny roadside shop. Hours are irregular, but you're pretty likely to find Wally there; or write to Box 177B, Route 4, South Danbury 03230; call (603) 768–5569.

The English House bed and breakfast in Andover is a little bit of Victorian Surrey transplanted. Its seven guest rooms, two of which are exceptionally large, have private baths, and two share a dormer sitting room with a window seat. This is only one example of the delightful architectural features of this meticulously restored turn-of-the-century home. Its British owners serve a classic full-course English breakfast with an international touch to the dishes, such as a Lebanese fruit compote. Proprietor Gillian Smith loves to share her considerable cooking talents with appreciative guests. Be sure to arrive in time for tea in the parlor.

Along with cooking and welcoming guests, Gillian offers classes in Polymer clay jewelry making. Cross-country enthusiasts can ski out of the back yard onto a series of well-groomed trails maintained by neighboring Procter Academy. Rental skis are available only 200 yards away in the village. Ask for the Smiths' map of local antiques shops—five of the shops specialize in old books and one in old maps. In fact, The English House maintains a miniature travel office in the guests' lounge, with scrapbooks full of ideas for the guests' entertainment. Write The English House, P.O. Box 162, Andover 03216 or call (603) 735–5987.

La Meridiana in Wilmot is a family-owned restaurant dedicated to the foods of the chef's home in northern Italy. Specialties include a salad of tender calamari, osso buco, gnocchi in a sauce so good that you'll be tempted to mop up the excess with the crusty Italian bread, and tender white veal with lemon served with lightly poached finocchi. The choice of desserts is equally varied and tempting: chocolate truffles, tiramisu, raspberry-chocolate cheesecake, zuppa inglese, canoli, or a traditional chocolate sponge cake with ricotta filling. Prices on all courses are inexpensive to moderate, with two-thirds of the entrées under $10.00. The wine list is quite reasonably priced as well. An especially endearing feature is that they suggest sharing a pasta course, so those without a gargantuan appetite can split a dish of risotto, gnocchi, or agnolotti as a first course and still have room for the entrée to follow. La Meridiana is on Route 11 and Old Winslow Road in Wilmot; call (603) 526–2033.

New London is the home of **Colby-Sawyer College,** whose stately campus dominates the southern end of the town's main street. Throughout the school year theater and musical performances keep the local arts scene lively, and then a summer theater takes over the job with Broadway musicals. The town is a good center for hiking and skiing; hikers and walkers can choose from among eight or nine trails leading to or past such varied attractions as a cave, a quarry, cascades, a beaver pond, abandoned farms, and lovely mountain views.

◆ **The Philbrick-Cricenti Bog,** a pond grown in with sphagnum moss, is located just out of the center of town. It is a fascinating nature reserve where you can observe the unique bog flora from wooden walkways, designed to protect both the fragile flora and your shoes. It's hard to see the trail sign from the road; look for the widened shoulder on the right after you pass Cricenti's Market. The trail is across the road.

Largely because of the college, the town abounds with places to eat. The dining room at the **New London Inn** offers a seasonally changing menu emphasizing local ingredients, such as an appetizer of pistachio-crusted goat cheese from neighboring Nunsuch Dairy. The current chef trained at the Hanover Inn and brings with him some of their flair for creative marriages of different cuisines, combining, for example, roasted peppers and Gorgonzola as a filling for wontons. Dinner is served daily in the summer and fall, daily except Sunday and Monday the rest of the year. Entrées range from $15.00 to $20.00.

Quiet lodgings await at the **Jonathan Hunting House B&B,** a fine old home set amid carefully tended gardens, surrounded by meadows red with Indian paintbrush and a maple forest to cool even the warmest summer day. Write to RR2, Box 780, New London 03257 or call (603) 526–9339. It's on Shaker Road, which turns off Route 11 to the east of New London. At the intersection, look for **Colonial Farm Inn & Antiques.** You probably won't find rare Hepplewhite pieces here, but you will see an interesting collection displayed with charm. You will also find a menu at the inn that may include wild mushroom soup or scallops with saf-

M/V *Mount Sunapee II*

fron. The Colonial Inn Farm, P.O. Box 1053, New London 03257; (603) 526–6121 or (800) 805–8504.

Although spring-fed ◆**Lake Sunapee** was a very popular resort area in the late 1800s, its shores have never been scoured by bulldozers or scarred by development. The only way to see the fine Victorian cottages nestled among the trees here is from the water. The **M/V *Mount Sunapee II*** takes passengers on an hour-and-a-half-long cruise along the 10-mile length of the lake, a tour made even more interesting by the intelligent and good-humored narration about the lake's history and lore. From the boat you can see Sunapee's three lighthouses, said to be the only ones on a New England lake. From mid-May to Columbus Day, the boat sails Saturday and Sunday at 2:30 P.M.; in addition, between mid-June and Labor Day it sails daily at 10:00 A.M. and 2:30 P.M. from Sunapee Harbor. For reservations write P.O. Box 345, Sunapee 03782 or call (603) 763–4030.

For a taste of the days of the grand hotels, dine aboard the **M/V *Kearsarge,*** a replica of the early lake steamers that brought guests from the train station to their lodgings. The Kearsarge's Victorian interior sets the stage for a buffet supper served during the summer sailings from Sunapee Harbor at 5:30 and 7:45 each evening. For reservations call (603) 763–5477.

Until the 1930s, the Woodsum family operated a fleet of steam passenger ships on Lake Sunapee. The ◆ **Sunapee Historical Museum** displays the pilot house of one of these rescued when the 70-foot SS *Kearsarge,* built in 1897, sank in 1935. Memorabilia of that golden age, including the handmade steam engine of a horseless carriage made in Newport in 1869, a milk delivery wagon, an 1824 fire pumper, an intact eighteenth-century dugout canoe, shop signs, and even a wooden water pipe, fill the museum. Plans are underway to restore the Woodsum Bros. machine shop. The museum is open 1:00 to 5:00 P.M. Tuesday through Sunday and 7:00 to 9:00 P.M. Wednesdays during July and August; weekends only in the spring and fall. It is at the landing in Sunapee Harbor; telephone (603) 763–2101.

Across the street at **Bob Skinners** and at **Alden of Sunapee,** kayaks, canoes, and paddle boats are available for daily or hourly rental. Each place has only one canoe, so making a reservation is wise. Call the former outfitter at (603) 763–9880 and the latter at (603) 763–3177. And if all this activity makes you hungry, you can have lunch (or breakfast) overlooking the lake on the porch of **The Anchorage,** where the menu offers Jamaican jerked wings, fried clams, "chowdah," pasta, burgers, and other choices. If you arrive by boat, they have their own slips for your use (603–763–3334).

Just up the hill from the docks, on Maple Street, **Haus Edel-weiss** offers a warm welcome with reasonably priced rooms and hearty Bavarian (or Yankee, if you prefer) breakfasts. Write to them at P.O. Box 609, Sunapee 03782 or call (603) 763–2100 or (800) 248–0713.

Late in the nineteenth century, New Hampshire promoted the re-use of abandoned farms as summer homes for the wealthy.

John Hay, Secretary to Abraham Lincoln, acquired ❖ **The Fells** in Newbury, at the southern tip of Lake Sunapee, in 1888. After his death, his son Clarence and his wife created extensive gardens on the property overlooking the lake. The rock garden covers both sides of a gently falling ravine and includes a stone Japanese lantern presented to Hay for his role in the Treaty of Portsmouth in 1905; a small stream flows through the ravine into a rock-lined lily pond before continuing into the forest below. The rose and perennial beds are in more formal terraced gardens, and an easy trail to the lake features placards with nature notes. On Route 103A between New London and Newbury, The Fells is open 10:00 A.M. to 6:00 P.M. weekends from late May through Labor Day. Contact NH Division of Parks and Recreation, P.O. Box 295, Newbury 03255; telephone (603) 763–2452.

Newbury's **Center Meeting House** was originally built about 1821, but was disassembled and rebuilt on its present site in 1832. A Bulfinch-inspired design, it has a unique interior arrangement; the box pews of the congregation face the entry doors (which would surely discourage late arrivals). The finely executed woodwork of the pulpit is supported by four columns and reached by a double staircase. Sunday services during July and August are at 11:00 A.M.

Railroads were important to the future of small towns when the line to Newbury was built in 1871. To complete it, the engineers had to excavate a massive trench, the **Newbury Cut,** through a solid granite hilltop using nitroglycerin to blast and strong backs to move the rubble, a process that took a year. Although the trains haven't run since 1961, you can get to the still-impressive cut in a leisurely twenty-minute walk along the old railbed, now a level birch-lined path alongside a marsh. Park at the town landing, just across the Route 103 intersection from the Meeting House, and look for the wide trail behind the small shopping center.

UPPER VALLEY

The town of Hanover and **Dartmouth College** are clustered around a large green, decorated in winter by a giant ice sculpture if the weather cooperates. Overlooking this from a slight hill are the white buildings of the original college. Two of the remaining sides are lined with red brick college buildings, among them

Baker library. The south side is divided between the Hanover Inn and the Hopkins Center for the Performing Arts. In and around that quadrangle lies an amazing wealth of art.

In the basement of ◆ **Baker Memorial Library** is a series of frescoes completed in 1934 by the Mexican artist José Clemente Orozco. A free brochure describing the frescoes is available at the central desk. They are powerful, and since their recent cleaning and restoration, true to their original brilliant colors. They were quite controversial in the 1930s but are now appreciated as a rare art treasure. Even less well known is the Hickmott **Shakespeare Collection,** also housed at Baker Library in the special collections room, open 8:00 A.M. to 4:30 P.M. Monday through Friday. The collection includes all four of the folio editions, close to forty quarto editions, all of the pre-1700 editions of *Macbeth,* and many other early editions. In the library's treasure room is Daniel Webster's set of John James Audubon's *Birds of America* in a folio first edition, more than 150 titles of incunabula (works printed before 1501), a 1439 Bible, and a collection of more than 200 volumes illustrating the art of fine book binding.

Adjoining the Hopkins Center is the new ◆ **Hood Museum of Art,** containing galleries for collections of American, European, African, Indian, and ancient art. The collection of Assyrian reliefs from the ninth century B.C. is rivaled in New England by only one other series. At the other end of history, the Hood is one of the very few American museums to own the entire suite of Picasso's Vollard etchings. There are Roman mosaics, paintings of the Italian Renaissance, baroque period, and Hudson River school, and representative pieces from every major style and period. Traveling exhibits often incorporate pieces from Dartmouth's own collections.

In 1991 the museum acquired the most comprehensive collection of Melanesian art in the country. Nearly 1,000 objects from Papua New Guinea and Vanuatu, ranging in size from miniatures to monumental works more than 8 feet tall, form a collection both comprehensive and rich in detail. Even with its new building, the museum cannot display everything, so inquire if you are interested in a particular subject. Temporary special exhibitions change twice each Dartmouth term. Open all year, Tuesday through Saturday 10:00 A.M. to 5:00 P.M. and Sunday 12:00 noon to 4:00 P.M. You can write for information to The Hood Museum, On the Green, Hanover 03755, or call (603) 646–2808.

The **Hopkins Center** is as broad in its offerings of performing arts as the Hood is in the fine arts. Telephone (603) 646–2422.

◆ **The Hanover Inn** is an institution almost as revered as Dartmouth College itself. Whenever the inn changes so much as a carpet, some old grad notices and comments. That has not stopped the inn from undertaking renovations to keep it up to date with modern amenities such as phones with modem ports. As the oldest continuously operated business in New Hampshire, the inn treads a careful balance between maintaining its historical flavor and providing luxurious accommodations and service that anticipates every need. Rooms are elegant, some with real marble baths. In the Daniel Webster Room's carpeted pink and gray Edwardian setting, Chef Michael Gray presents a menu as understated and elegant as the decor. Dinner may begin with an appetizer of delicately smoked tender scallops, then proceed to veal or a tuna steak served with shrimp dumplings. Flavors and textures are perfectly balanced in dishes that blend the nuances of a variety of cuisines. In short, the dining room is worthy of the hotel. Open for lunch and for dinner, Tuesday through Sunday, its address is: On The Green, Hanover 03755; telephone (800) 443–7024.

If you are a celebrity watcher, you can get the autograph of those performing or speaking at the Hopkins Center by waiting in the corridor that connects it with the inn. They all stay at the inn and use this private lower-level passageway before and after appearances. Expect to pay well for rooms in this top-rated hotel, but also expect to get your money's worth. Write The Hanover Inn, On the Green, Hanover 03755; call (603) 643–4300 or (800) 443–7024.

In an unimposing corner storefront facing the common in nearby Lebanon, **Sweet Tomatoes Trattoria** has quickly become a mecca (or should we say Bologna?) for lovers of real Italian food. From their wood-fired oven emerge roasted eggplant for caponata, roasted mushrooms for antipasto, and roasted chicken and peppers for several dishes, not to mention an array of pizzas, many topped with wood-roasted vegetables. We have, in the past year, ordered everything on their substantial menu at least once, from the linguine with calamari to the marinated chicken grilled with herbs, and our favorite is always the one that's just been set in front of us. Entrée prices are under $10.00 and wines are sold by the glass or by the bottle. Portions are generous, service personal, and the atmosphere upbeat and relaxed. Sweet Tomatoes is at One Court Street, Lebanon 03766; telephone (603) 448–1711.

The ◆ **Lower Shaker Village** at Enfield, while not as extensive as the one at Canterbury, is of special interest for its stone architecture. The largest Shaker dwelling house in existence, four and one-half stories tall, is now the Shaker Inn, which has a restaurant downstairs and inexpensive guest accommodations in the austere upper floors. These rooms have the sparse simplicity and built-in cabinets that are hallmarks of Shaker design. Write The Shaker Inn, Enfield 03748 or call (603) 632–5466.

The museum portion is best known for its herb gardens and for the regular series of workshops in Shaker arts, industries, and gardening held there throughout the year. In early June, a Festival of Shaker Crafts and Herbs features plants, herbal and Shaker crafts, demonstrations, and programs on herb gardening and cooking. Open June 1 to October 15, Monday through Saturday, 10:00 A.M. to 5:00 P.M., Sunday 12:00 noon to 5:00 P.M., and weekends only through the winter. It's on Route 4A in Enfield; call (603) 632–4346 for more information.

Northwest from the village of Canaan is the unusual settlement of ◆ **Canaan Street.** The main, and only, street is lined on both sides with a mile of distinguished white homes and churches. These date from as early as 1794. Behind the single row of homes on the east is a lake, and in the other direction is a sweeping view over the valley to the Green Mountains of Vermont. Wide lawns surround the homes, and the broad street is lined with maples and stone walls. The entire scene, so unexpectedly encountered, seems to have been dropped there from the last century. The last house on the left is **The Inn on Canaan Street,** one of the quietest and most lovingly managed of New Hampshire's many small inns. Breakfast here always features fresh-baked scones or muffins. Rooms are large, bright, and comfortable; prices are moderate. Write to them at Box 92, Canaan Street, Canaan 03741; or call (603) 523–7310.

On Route 118, 3 miles from the center of Canaan, Dan Allen of **Highland Meadow Wood Carvings** creates wood sculptures, including 12-foot-long life-size moose, and larger-than-life animals, such as the appealing squirrel in the front yard. A 3-foot garden gnome, reading a book while perched on a mushroom, is about $65.00, while smaller figures are less. There is no sign, but look for a pile of logs across from the house and examples of Allen's work on the lawn. Write to him at RFD 2, Box 19, Canaan 03741 or call (603) 523–7291. After you've been here you'll recognize his work adorning area businesses.

BAKER RIVER AND NEWFOUND LAKE

New Hampshire is filled with stone profiles, and although none rivals the fame of the Old Man of the Mountains in Franconia Notch, each has its degree of local renown. Some require a great deal of imagination or at least a view from the right spot to distinguish. ◆**Profile Falls,** 2½ miles south of Bristol on Route 3A, demands both imagination and the right view, but even without spotting the profile, the falls themselves are well worth the short walk. Turn off Route 3A to the east (left if you're traveling south) just before the bridge with the small sign for the falls. A short distance down that road is another small sign and a pullout area on the right, but it is steep and slippery, so we suggest parking along the road just before the sign. Follow the road to the trail or follow the snowmobile trail, which also leads to the base of the falls. The drop is about 40 feet over a broad ledge, and the profile is supposed to be at the foot of the falls in silhouette against the white water. On hot days, local boys can often be found jumping from the high rocks on the right into the pool at the base of the falls. We don't recommend that you try this.

North of Bristol on Route 3A is a picnic area maintained by the Rotary Club, in a grove of pines. Shortly past this a road leads to West Shore Road, which hugs the shore of Newfound Lake and offers lovely views of the lake and mountains. Along the road, on a point of land surrounded by the unusually clear waters of the lake, is one of New Hampshire's finest and perhaps least known beaches. ◆**Wellington State Park** has a fine sandy beach under tall pines, so you can choose sun or shade and still be at the water's edge. You can't launch boats from the park, but you can put in canoes or small sailing craft easily. It is a busy, friendly park with plenty of beach and water, so it never seems crowded. It's open 9:00 A.M. to 8:00 P.M. on weekends from Memorial Day to the last week of June and for the two weeks after Labor Day. During the rest of the summer it's open daily from 9:00 A.M. to 8:00 P.M.

At the northern end of the lake, between the attractive village of Hebron and Route 3A, is the **Hebron Marsh Wildlife Sanctuary.** You can park down the dirt road just before the red cottage while you visit the diverse wildlife habitats of freshwater marsh, open fields, and the banks of the Cockermouth River. Follow signs to the southwest corner of the field to find the short trail leading to the observation tower. From here you can look out over the marsh and see wood ducks, buffleheads, pied-billed grebes, great blue herons, osprey, beaver, and perhaps moose and loons. Songbirds abound, and the trail through the fields gives a closer view of the wildflowers.

Only 1¼ miles down the road is the ◆**Paradise Point Nature Center** (look sharp to find its sign on the downhill side of the road next to the driveway). In addition to the trails through an unspoiled lakeshore of coniferous forest, the center includes hands-on exhibits, a library, bird-viewing area, and a fascinating audio-aided exhibit demonstrating the various calls of the loon. A full schedule of naturalist programs is offered, including a sunrise canoe trip. Before walking the trails, be sure to pick up the free visitors guide, with descriptions of the natural history and inhabitants of the area. Try to spot the tupelo tree, rarely found in New England, as you walk alongside the swamp on the Elwell Trail. Its horizontal branches are covered in brilliant red leaves in the fall. The center is open weekends 10:00 A.M. to 4:00 P.M. in the spring and fall and daily 10:00 A.M. to 5:00 P.M. from the last week in June to Labor Day. There is no admission fee, but the Audubon Society, which operates the center, is always grateful for donations to help them continue their work of acquiring and protecting natural habitats. Write Audubon Society of New Hampshire, North Shore Road, East Hebron 03232 or call (603) 744–3516.

Going west from Hebron through Groton, a road leads to ◆**Sculptured Rocks.** About a mile from the turnoff, watch for a signpost, although the sign may not be there during the off-season. You'll see a parking area on the left, and the chasm is on the right side of the road. The river here has carved its way under granite boulders, leaving only the crowns of some and forming giant potholes in others that appear to have been the work of a giant ice cream scoop. Below the bridge a trail leads past falls, pools and huge moss-covered boulders, culminating in a sheer rock cliff on one side. Notice the full-grown trees on the side walls with their roots gripping the walls like fingers.

The back road through Groton and North Rumney is a seldom-traveled alternative to Route 3A. The town of Rumney sits off of Route 25, spread around a central common. Quilt enthusiasts should stop at the Calico Cupboard for a wide selection of fabrics, supplies, and books (603–786–9567).

Quincy Road, which goes off the far end of Rumney's village green, will take you to ◆ **The Quincy Bog.** Exactly 2 miles from the village green you will see stone pillars on either side of a small road to the left. Down this road $\frac{1}{10}$th mile there is another left, which ends shortly at the bog entrance. Nature trails and a viewing deck offer a look at rare bog plants and a wetland ecosystem different from those of shores and marshes. The best months to see the bog plants in bloom are May and June.

On the way to Quincy bog you will pass the most unusual ◆ **Town Pound** in the state. While pounds were usually made of four sturdy stone walls, forming a square, with a gate on one side, the townspeople of old Rumney took advantage of a geological feature as interesting as the pound itself. Huge boulders, which appear to have fallen from the cliffs above, lie in a great tumble. Two of them form protected cavelike areas, and two others form straight walls. By adding only one and a half sides and a gate, the town created a fine enclosure for stray animals, one that even offered shelter from rain and wind. Climb through the space in the center of the back and you'll find a trail through an arch formed by two huge boulders. You can climb farther and wander amid these granite giants. The pound is a fascinating combination of natural and human history. You'll see one wall of the pound directly across the road from the immense boulder that sits almost in the road.

Leaving Rumney on Main Street you will pass an extraordinary garden where visitors are welcome. **Mr. Jacquith's Garden** seems to be in bloom all the time, with a succession of flowers set in showy beds along the road. A place of visual delight, this work of one man rivals the loveliest show gardens anywhere. There is no admission fee, but you'll see a box for donations to help with the expense of replacing plants, and you'll probably want to add something to it. Although Mr. Jacquith is no longer living, his son and daughter-in-law, who run the plant nursery next door, have maintained his garden. At the nursery is a charming small perennial garden, and they sell herb and flower plants from their greenhouse, and fresh vegetables at their farmstand.

The road past these gardens leads to Stinson Lake. Along the way is the **Mary Baker Eddy House.** The founder of the Christian Science faith lived here in the early 1860s. The house is open Tuesday through Saturday 10:00 A.M. to 5:00 P.M. and Sunday 2:00 to 5:00 P.M. May through October. From here a guide will also take you to another Eddy home in North Groton. The road, which turns to gravel, continues to climb through the woods. Watch for a waterfall to the left just as you cross a bridge. Farther on, as you top the ridge, you will have sweeping views into the White Mountain National Forest, just a teaser for the views you will have as you continue north.

If your taste for travel doesn't run to dirt roads you can go north from Rumney through the National Forest along Route 118 or take Route 25 to Plymouth, a short distance away. On the way to Plymouth on this route you'll see **Glory Jean's,** a shiny O'Mahoney diner built in 1954. It's the real thing inside, too, with '50s tunes on the jukebox and diner favorites like hot turkey sandwiches, meatloaf, bread pudding, and homemade pies. Call the diner at (603) 786–2352.

Not far south of Glory Jean's is **The Crabapple Inn Bed & Breakfast,** in a beautiful 1835 Federal-style home. As well-restored inside as out, the inn provides such luxuries as a canopied four-poster bed in a room whose private bathroom is large enough to be a guest room. Handmade quilts, antique furnishings, mountain views, herb and perennial gardens, and the choice of an elegant dining room or a bricked terrace as a setting for breakfast are just a few of the touches here. The rates are a little higher than at many B&Bs (they begin at $75.00 per couple), but this is an elegant and comfortable home. Write to the inn at RR 4, Box 1955, Plymouth 03264, or call (603) 536–4476.

You won't have an easy time finding **The Backyard Trattoria** in Plymouth, since it's down an alley behind (and under) the Trolley Stop. The menu is rich in Italian favorites. The chef's specials change daily and may include such mouth-watering choices as delicately herbed shrimp with artichokes, chicken breast Marsala, or tender fettucini in a rich (but not heavy) Alfredo sauce. Desserts are . . . let us just say that their *tiramisu* is better than any we ever had in Italy, and we've sampled this treat from Lugano to Sicily. Dinner is served from 5:00 to 9:00 P.M. every night during summer and foliage season; call for schedules the rest of the year. The Backyard seats only twenty-nine in its bright and cozy dining room (603) 536–1994.

THE LAKES AND FOOTHILLS

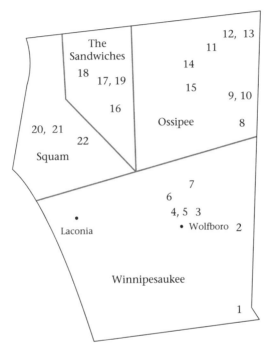

1. New Hampshire Farm
   Museum
2. Museum of Childhood
3. Wentworth Park
4. Clark House Museum
   Complex
5. M/V *Doris E*
6. Abenaki Tower
7. Dow's Corner Shop
8. The Effiinghams
9. Freedom Historical Society
10. Fairfield Llama Farm
11. Madison Boulder
12. Snow Village Inn
13. Bike the Whites
14. White Lake State Park
15. Summer Brook Trout Farm
16. The Old Country Store
17. Sandwich Historical Society
    Museum
18. Sandwich Notch
19. The Corner House
20. The Sailing Center
21. Science Center of New
    Hampshire
22. Red Hill Inn

THE LAKES AND FOOTHILLS

North of the Merrimack Valley and the seacoast regions lies an area of rolling farmlands and small mountains. The northernmost of these are the foothills of the White Mountains beyond.

In the center lies Lake Winnipesaukee, an enormous body of water surrounded by several other sizable lakes. The southern shores of Winnipesaukee are covered with popular tourist paths and filled with man-made "attractions" and cheek-by-jowl resorts. While there are some lovely, quiet pockets in this area, it is generally too well known and too heavily trodden to be of interest in this book.

Instead, we shall explore the eastern shore of Lake Winnepesaukee and other lakes east of I-91 and the mountains and forests that border them. Ossipee, Wentworth, Squam, Silver, and Province lakes are joined by innumerable smaller ones providing reflecting pools for some of the state's prettiest villages. We won't name or take you past all of them, so you should explore the back roads to discover some of them for yourselves. Country inns, covered bridges, rock-lined brooks, and old farms lie along back roads here, and at the crossroads are villages that date from the earliest days of the colony.

WINNIPESAUKEE

Memories of New Hampshire's early agriculture are displayed and used at the ◆New Hampshire Farm Museum on Plummer's Ridge, just north of Milton. Housed in the state's best-preserved series of connected farm buildings (the house and barn are connected by a series of buildings and sheds to facilitate winter access and farm chores), the museum began as a simple collection of early implements. In addition to the house and barn (the latter is filled with fascinating old tools and equipment) there are blacksmith and cobbler shops. Special weekend events illustrating early farm life include days featuring herbs, dairy farming, fibers, farm animals, and other subjects. The second Saturday in August is Old Time Farm Day, with more than sixty demonstrations of farming skills and crafts. Open mid-June to Labor Day Tuesday through Saturday 10:00 a.m. to 4:00 p.m., Sundays 12:00 noon to 4:00 p.m., and on weekends for the same hours in the fall. Admission is $5.00 for adults, $1.50 for children. Write New Hampshire Farm

Museum, Route 125, P.O. Box 644, Milton 03851 or call (603) 652–7840. In 1995, the adjacent Plummer homestead, another fine collection of connected buildings, becomes a living, working, 1890s farm, providing an even fuller view of nineteenth-century farm life.

For most of the nineteenth century, **Wakefield Corner** was an important stop on the route north, but then it lost its position to Sanbornville's rail junction. Since then, it has stayed so close to its nineteenth-century appearance that the entire village has been named a historic district. Its white wooden houses sit in gracious fence-encircled yards, and features such as the hay scales and horse trough are still standing. A Rails-to-Trails project is in progress, converting the former railbed into a hiking and biking path from Wakefield to Wolfeboro.

The innkeepers of **The Wakefield Inn** have prepared a booklet describing the architecture and the buildings in town, which they lend to guests who wish to take a walking tour. That's only one of the reasons for staying at this three-and-a-half-story Federal-style inn. The rooms are large, airy, and beautifully decorated, all with private baths. Dinners, served on weekends to guests with prior reservation only, may feature chicken breast with cornbread stuffing, crab-stuffed filet of sole, or shrimp baked in puff pastry. Historical features such as original window glass, a three-sided fireplace, and Indian shutters make the inn as interesting as it is hospitable; guests enjoy gathering to share their day's travel experiences around the glass-fronted woodstove. Write the inn at Mt. Laurel Road, Route 1, Box 2185, Wakefield 03872; telephone (603) 522–8272 or (800) 245–0841.

A few doors up the street is the ◆**Museum of Childhood.** Two sisters, Marjorie Banks and Elizabeth MacRury, have collected dolls and toys both at home and on their frequent foreign travels. When the collection threatened to engulf their home, they purchased a house a few doors away, and the museum was born. More than 3,000 dolls, from puppets to clothes-pin dolls, inhabit the rooms, along with teddy bears, sleds, and a *complete* 1890s schoolroom. The collectors, who are happy to accompany visitors and bring these bits of childhood memories alive, are as delightful as the collection. Everyone leaves smiling, especially children, who can't resist the stories. "Sara is visiting her grandmother in Tuftonboro today, but she won't mind your looking in her room," Elizabeth assures a young visitor. Open May through October,

81

Wednesday through Monday 11:00 A.M. to 4:00 P.M., except Sunday 1:00 to 4:00 P.M. The Museum of Childhood is on Mt. Laurel Road in Wakefield; call (603) 522–8073 for more information.

Despite all the lakes around, finding a public place to swim can be difficult. ◆ **Wentworth Park** on Route 109 between Wakefield and Wolfeboro is a small beach with bathhouses and a picnic area along its sandy shorefront. Nearby is the stone foundation and well of the summer estate of Benning Wentworth, first of New Hampshire's royal governors. This 100-by-40-foot structure with stories 18 feet high and windows 6 feet tall is thought to have been the first summer vacation "cottage" in America, built in 1768. Unfortunately, the estate burned not long after the Revolution. In the summer there is often an archeological dig here.

Wolfeboro's Main Street is busy in the summer, but there is a leisurely air here, with no traffic jams. For a good lunch in a local, friendly atmosphere, stop at the **Mast Landing Restaurant** at the bridge in the middle of town. It's a classic, with blue painted booths, waitresses who chat with you, and daily specials on a bulletin board over the pie case (featuring apple, blueberry, pumpkin, apricot, cherry, lemon meringue, and chocolate custard). It's not the place for an intimate tête-à-tête, but it's lively, friendly, and reliable. Open daily until 3:00 P.M. for breakfast and lunch only; breakfast is served all day. Call ahead for take-out lunches (603–569–1789).

In the winter, **Nordic Skier** on North Main Street offers 20 kilometers of well-groomed and tracked cross-country with lake views. This complete center offers equipment rentals and lessons (603–569–3151).

The Wolfeboro Historical Society operates the ◆ **Clark House Museum Complex,** which includes a replica of a mid-nineteenth-century firehouse, an 1868 schoolhouse, and an eighteenth-century farmhouse. Open Monday through Saturday 10:00 A.M. to 4:00 P.M. in July and August. It's on South Main Street in Wolfeboro; call (603) 569–4997 or 569–3667.

An interesting two-hour cruise of the islands on the east side of Lake Winnipesaukee leaves from Wolfeboro on Saturdays and Sundays at 10:00 A.M., 12:00 noon, and 2:00 P.M. and Friday and Saturday evenings at 6:30 P.M. The captain of the ◆ **M/V Doris E** points out interesting features on shore and enlivens the cruise with local stories and history. Light refreshments are available, but if you would like to enjoy a glass of wine with the sunset, you'll have to bring your own. The fare is $8.00 for adults and $4.00 for children. For details call (603) 366–2628.

The ◆**Abenaki Tower,** a little farther along Route 109 in Melvin Village, gives no clue to its origin except the date of its construction. This sturdy wooden structure puts you above the treetops for a 180-degree view over Lake Winnipesaukee and its wooded islands and bays. The Belknap Mountains back it to the south and the Squam Range to the north. It's a short easy walk and then a stiff climb, but the view is spectacular, especially at sunset. Notice the unusual raised lines on the boulder near the trail.

Although there are antiques shops all over the state, some of which come and go within a season or two, there is one in Tuftonboro that is well worth a visit. ◆**Dow's Corner Shop** has occupied its enormous barn for close to fifty years. It is so full of antiques that you have to walk sideways in the narrow aisles. From export china to 1920s fur coats, if you collect it, they'll not only have it, but they will have several to choose from. This is also a good place to find the once popular Kilburn stereoscopic view cards of New Hampshire. Open daily May 1 to October 15 and by chance in the winter. Dow's Corner Shop is on Route 171 at Tuftonboro Corner, R.F.D. Ossipee 03864; (603–539–4790).

Not far from there, on Route 28 in Wolfeboro, is **Bittersweet,** whose barn dining room is decorated with utensils, implements, pottery, china, quilts, and old sheet music from area antiques stores. All of these are for sale, with discreet price tags affixed. The interesting decor should not take your attention away from the menu, which presents a lively collection of entrées including lamb and cider pie, Wiener schnitzel, and chicken parmigiana. Whatever you choose, don't miss the spinach salad with hot bacon dressing. Open May to December, serving dinner Monday through Saturday, 5:00 P.M. to 9:00 P.M., and Sunday brunch buffet 11:00 A.M. to 2:00 P.M. (603–569–3636).

OSSIPEE

Unlike New Hampshire's western border, where the Connecticut River makes a clean separation with Vermont, the border with Maine, north of Wakefield, is merely a surveyor's line. Roads and villages that grew up prior to this line sprawl and meander from one side to the other. Route 153 is one of these, not only a lovely road to travel, but a good alternative for shunpikers seeking to avoid the traffic of Route 16. On its way to Conway, this road weaves through valleys and around the shores of little lakes. Province Lake nudges it over the line into Maine for a few miles until it re-enters New Hampshire at South Effingham.

◆ **The Effinghams,** and there are four of them, were once a very prosperous community based on a group of mills built along the Ossipee River in the 1820s. Center Effingham overlooks the road from a hill, with an imposing town hall that doubles as a Masonic Lodge. That accounts for the emblem on the clock face. A grange hall, a church, and several homes complete the historic village.

To the north is Effingham, also known as Lord's Hill. This cluster of early nineteenth-century buildings includes a church, a 1780s hip-roofed house, and several impressive homes of 1820s origin. Just down from the crest of the hill is a road with a historic marker describing the Effingham Union Academy, New Hampshire's first state teachers college. A short distance up that road, set among manicured lawns and huge shade trees, is **Squire Lord's mansion.** For its size and the quality of its architecture, this would be an impressive building in Portsmouth or Exeter. Here, come upon suddenly in such a rural setting, it is astonishing. Its three stories rise in clean lines, the eye drawn upward to the tall, octagonal, domed cupola. A Palladian window in the second floor surmounts the wide Federal doorway. No longer open for public tours, the mansion is now a private home. Please respect this and continue down the road a few yards to the academy to turn around.

The town of Freedom lies along a small river, its two streets lined by fine homes, many with interesting decorative trim. On Maple Street is the ◆ **Freedom Historical Society,** whose collections include furnished rooms. The Victorian parlor is particularly illustrative of life in these prosperous mill towns during their heyday, with its ornate fainting couch and stereoscope viewer. Open Tuesday, Thursday, Saturday, and Sunday, 2:00 to 4:00 P.M. Just down the street is the **Freedom House Bed and Breakfast,** in a beautifully restored Victorian home. The guest rooms are bright and spotless country style, with nice decorative

Fairfield Llama Farm

detail. It is open year-round, and you'll have to reserve early to stay there during the town's annual Old Home Week in August. Write Freedom House Bed and Breakfast, Maple Street, Freedom 03836; call (603) 539–4815.

◆**Fairfield Llama Farm,** which you would expect to find in the surrounding farmland, is along the main street of the village, close to its neighbors. In the wide, sloping backyard live a small herd of the shaggy, irresistible creatures, their faces set in a perpetual grin. Deborah Frock will take you on leisurely treks with llamas carrying your lunch, cameras, and nature guides. The soft foot of the llama does no harm to woodlands, and hiking with one alerts you to the many pleasures of the forest. Deborah's favorite trek is to the summit of Foss Mountain, where there is a 360-degree view of Maine and New Hampshire as far as Mount

Washington. This half-day trip can be made late in the day, in time to enjoy dessert (see below), along with the sunset, at the summit and be back by dark. Write for reservations (she'll call you to confirm) at P.O. Box 96, Freedom 03836.

If you're staying at **Purity Spring Resort,** they'll pack an elegant dessert for you to carry along on your llama trek. But be sure to check their evening schedule, since you don't want to miss their Thursday lobster and steak cookout on their private island. Each day at this casual family resort brings new activities, from a Monday morning breakfast cooked over a campfire to the Friday night steamship smorgasbord. The dining room in the old-fashioned American-plan resort offers a choice of five entrées each evening, always including a meatless alternative. Non-guests are welcome at meals—some families come every week for the lobster cookout.

Everything here is included: day care, tennis, canoes, rowboats, and all outdoor activities, except an all-day canoe trip on the nearby Saco River. Grandparents who first came here as children are still returning to this comfortable, homey resort. It is also handicapped accessible. Write them at East Madison 03849; telephone (800) 367–8897 from the United States or Canada.

King Pine Ski Area just up the road is small, but it has trails for those of all skill levels. Six trails and slopes are lighted for night skiing. Facilities are up to date, but prices are old-fashioned and made even better with joint ski-lodging packages with Purity Spring. A complete ski school and the relaxed atmosphere of King Pine make it a particular favorite of families. It's located on Route 153 in East Madison; call (800) 367–8897.

The ◆**Madison Boulder,** off Route 113 between Conway and Madison, is the largest known example of a glacial erratic in New England, and one of the largest in the world. Enormous free-standing boulders are not uncommon in New Hampshire, but none even approaches the size of this 83-foot, 5,000-ton giant. This is not just another big rock. Such erratics were broken from large outcrops of granite by glaciers, then carried away and dropped in spots sometimes several miles distant. This one is thought to have come from cliffs about 4 miles away, but some geologists believe that it came from Mount Willard, 25 miles north in Crawford Notch.

Something is always happening at the ◆**Snow Village Inn,** a hillside retreat built in 1900 by the historian Frank Simonds.

Fellow guests may be dressed in outrageous outfits to play their roles in a murder mystery weekend, or be warming their hands and feet after a dogsled ride across frozen Crystal Lake behind the inn's friendly Samoyeds, Boris and Natasha. That's not to suggest that you can't just sit here and enjoy the view or the collection of early optical toys in the parlor; the inn is equally well-suited to inactivity. The best view in the house is from the second-floor Robert Frost room, with three walls of solid windows and a vista spanning from Mt. Chocorua to Maine, encompassing Mt. Washington and the Presidential Range, 30 miles north. The decor is elegant, but not overdone, with guests' comfort firmly in mind. Part of the fun of any inn should be the personality of its owners, and the lively Cutrones have plenty to spare. Food is Trudy's specialty and the dinners she serves reflect her Austrian heritage and fresh local ingredients. This superior inn is well worth its slightly above-moderate rates. For reservations write them at Snowville 03849 or call (603) 447–2818 or (800) 447–4345.

You can arrive at the Snow Village by bicycle (we'd walk it up the last steep hill to the inn) in a ❖ **Bike the Whites** package that includes a night here, one at the **Tamworth Inn,** and one at **The Forest Inn** (see p. 102). Beginning on Sundays, the tours include breakfasts and dinners, maps with points of interest noted, luggage transfers, transportation to the starting point, and emergency assistance if needed en route. For information, write The Tamworth Inn, Box 189, Tamworth 03886 or call (800) 933–3902.

Overlooking the postcard-perfect Crystal Lake in "downtown" Eaton, **The Inn at Crystal Lake** looks exactly like what it is—a hostelry that has welcomed travelers to this tiny village since the 1880s. Its three layers of porches, rows of rockers, and columned façade mark it even before you see the sign. Inside this period piece, simply-furnished rooms are comfortable and the menu surprisingly ambitious, offering a wide variety of choices (such as sautéed duckling breast and chicken with Brie) to inn guests and the public. Under new management in 1994, the inn retains its homey charms but reflects the style of the new innkeepers. Write them at Route 153, Eaton Center 03832; or call (603) 447–2120 or (800) 343–7336.

❖ **White Lake State Park** packs three attractions into one compact park that surrounds a crystal-clear lake. The lake's swimming beach stretches along one end, with the rest of the shore bordered in trees. A walking trail encircles its perimeter, and a campground offers well-spaced sites under tall pine trees, the forest floor padded by a soft carpet of pine needles. Across the lake is a stand of **pitch pines** that have been declared a National Natural Landmark. Close to the northern tip of their range, the pitch pines here are especially large, which indicates age, but they are hard to date because they don't grow even rings for each year's growth. Pitch pine trees have difficulty reproducing except after a forest fire, since their cones need the heat to spring them open and release the seeds. Open from the end of May to Columbus Day, White Lake is in Tamworth; call (603) 323–7350.

Another interesting pine-forest environment is located a short distance away along the road between Silver Lake and West Ossipee. The **West Branch Pine Barrens,** part of which is owned by the Nature Conservancy, is considered one of the world's finest examples of pine barrens. Its layer of birch and scrub oak grows under a canopy of pitch pine, with blueberry bushes closer to the ground. The barrens is home to several rare moth varieties that feed on its trees.

Just north of the village of Chocorua, you'll see a sign for the **Riverbend Country Inn** on the west side of Route 16. Although only a short distance from the traffic, it seems to be deep in the woods. The inn overlooks a deep curve in the Chocorua River, and in good weather guests have breakfast outside on a terrace that extends out over the riverbank. The inn is as lovely as its setting, with bright airy guest rooms and antiques-furnished public rooms. Little details, such as a kitchenette where tea and cookies are always available, make guests feel pampered. Write to the inn at P.O. Box 347, Chocorua 03817; call (603) 323–7440 or (800) 628–6944.

Don't be put off by the fear of looking like the two fat pink pigs on the sign of **The Yankee Smokehouse** at the intersection of Routes 16 and 25 in West Ossipee. This is an authentic open-pit barbecue, one of the few in New England. The service is so unremittingly cheerful and eager here that it reminds us of Disney World. Servers describe each specialty and suggest the best deal. "You'll get more of the same thing for less money by ordering the sampler for one and splitting it," our waiter once advised us after mentally toting up our order. Beef or pork ribs or slices, chicken, and delicious baby back pork ribs are their specialties, but you can have the sliced smoked beef or pork in a sandwich or the chicken made into a wonderful smoked salad. Don't miss the corn chowder (it's unlikely that your waiter will allow you to order a meal without it), which is solid with chunks of potato, bacon, and corn, seasoned with herbs and plenty of pepper. You can roll up your sleeves and eat until you can't hold another bite here and have trouble making the bill come out to $10.00 each. If you have a group of at least eight, order the Smokehouse Feast for $47.95. It says on the menu that it feeds four to six, but it's enough for a regiment on the march. Open all year, except April and from mid-November to mid-December (telephone 603–539–RIBS).

South of the Yankee Smokehouse on Route 16, a former state fish hatchery has been converted to ❖ **Summer Brook Fish Farm.** Fly-fishing enthusiasts can practice their skills in the pond on a catch-and-release basis, or those who prefer can catch their supper at 30 cents an inch. The farm also sells trout or will stock your own pond. Open weekends spring and fall, daily Memorial Day through Labor Day (603) 539–7232.

THE SANDWICHES

Some of New Hampshire's quirky private museums—collections gathered over the years by people with a particular hobby or interest—have signs by the roadside inviting people in, and some don't. Even when you're in ❖ **The Old Country Store,** at the crossroads in Moultonboro, you might not notice the sign by the stairs pointing to the museum. The whole upper floor is filled with local history—saws, axes, and other tools; a wooden snow shovel; blacksmithing tools; maple sugaring equipment; advertising cards; cigar store Indians; yarn winders—neatly labeled, often in some detail. There is no curator and no charge; you just wander around at your leisure. You might want to show your appreciation by taking home some common crackers or some cheddar cheese from the wheel in the glass case downstairs or stopping for a Moxie or a cream soda from the big old ice chest, but everybody's very pleasant even if you don't buy anything. Outside in the barn is an original Concord Coach that is thought to be the oldest Concord-built stagecoach in existence.

A good restaurant nearby is **The Sweetwater Inn** on Route 25, where they serve moderately priced northern Italian specialties such as fettucini with shrimp and scallops, ravioli filled with lobster, veal medallions with assorted mushrooms, and chicken with shrimp and a hazel nut liqueur (603–476–5079).

The Village of Center Sandwich is largely made up of houses built in the first half of the nineteenth century. The houses are clustered into a handful of tree-lined streets, an open invitation to stroll through town. Along with the antique and craft shops, be sure to stop at the ◆ **Sandwich Historical Society Museum.** Its furnishings include a kitchen, household implements, and a wide variety of artifacts from the town's eighteenth-century beginnings through the early twentieth century. Open, free of charge, Monday through Saturday, 11:00 A.M. to 5:00 P.M. in July and August and 1:00 to 5:00 P.M. June and September (603–284–6665).

Follow Grove Street and then bear left at road signs for ◆ **Sandwich Notch.** It is reached by a gravel road that is not maintained for winter use. The stone walls beside it once outlined the fields of farms, now overgrown into forests. A cart track, the road was put through the notch in 1801 as a route for north-country farmers to get their produce to the markets of Portsmouth and Portland and return with supplies and goods not produced on their own farms. Later bypassed by other routes, the road through this notch has not changed very much for the past century-and-a-half.

A parking area on the right marks the short trail to **Beede's Falls.** Where the trail meets the river, an island cuts the river into two small channels. To the right, the water slides over ledges and drops in a series of cascades into a moss-lined pool below. The wooded area at the bottom is surrounded by a tumble of boulders, some of which form caves and crevices. If you go upstream along the island, you will see the brook rushing through a foot-wide shoot. A short distance above that, the river flows down a ledge and then drops 40 feet into a sandy pool. More rocks lie in giant tumbles here, too. Some of these overhang enough to form a cave that, legend has it, sheltered a stray cow for an entire winter. Above the main falls there are two more cascades. Because there are no signs here, it would be easy to miss the main falls to the left and to assume the cascades downstream to be Beede's Falls.

Not far up the road, between two bridges over the Bearcamp River, is a cliff shaped like the prow of a ship. Called **Pulpit Rock,** it was used as a pulpit by a long-ago Quaker pastor. The head of the notch, 7 miles from the center of Center Sandwich Village, is marked by a small sign high up on a tree and not easy to see. For a well-written history of the notch, read *The Road Through Sandwich Notch* by Elizabeth Yates.

There are more entrées on the daily special blackboard at ◆**The Corner House** in Center Sandwich than most restaurants have on their printed menu. These dishes allow the chef to take advantage of ingredients with short seasons and the chance to serve his latest original dish. This might be a double lamb chop stuffed with a blend of ricotta, parmesan, and spinach. The printed menu is not ho-hum either, with such offerings as medallions of chicken breast stuffed with ham and artichoke hearts or veal smothered in chunks of lobster with broccoli and béarnaise sauce. A grinding of nutmeg on the cappuccino tops off a fine dinner here. Prices are moderate; lunch (try the crabcakes) is served every day except Sunday in the summer and on Wednesday through Saturday in the winter. Dinner is served every summer evening from 5:30 P.M. and Wednesday through Sunday in the winter.

Upstairs there are four moderately priced guest rooms decorated with a stylish Victorian flair. Furnishings include brass and oak beds, wicker chairs, hand-hooked rugs, spool towel racks, marble-topped bureaus, and prints that range from Godey's *Lady's Book* illustrations to French impressionist exhibition posters. Open year-round; write The Corner House, Box 204, Center Sandwich 03227 or call (603) 284–6219.

Squam

The quiet of Squam Lake is almost legendary. Its irregular shape, with bays, inlets, and islands, makes it virtually impossible for power boats to get up any speed, so there is very little to disturb the loons that nest there. Cottages along the shore are tucked behind the trees, giving it the feel of a wilderness lake. See it from the water in a canoe or sailboat rented at ◆**The Sailing Center** on Route 3 in Holderness. They offer Phantoms, Daysailers, kayaks, and 16-foot fiberglass canoes, complete with all safety equipment, as well as sailing lessons. Rates run from $15.00 for a half-day canoe rental to $55.00 for a 17-foot Daysailer. Full-day and weekly rentals bring the rates even lower. Call (603) 968–3233 to reserve a craft.

The ✦ **Science Center of New Hampshire** on Route 113 in Holderness encourages visitors to explore six different natural communities along its exhibit trail. Signs and staff members explain the ecosystems of the marsh, field, pond, stream, forest, and lake, showing how plants and animals live together in each setting. Signboards explore such questions as "If the marsh were drained, who would suffer?" The marsh community is reached by a boardwalk, often covered with little bodies lying on their stomachs watching painted turtles, leopard frogs, and trout below. Birds are everywhere, perched on fences or signposts or darting between trees. The setting is attractive and well maintained, a good way to understand the woods, fields, and waters as you travel around the state. Young travelers will enjoy the Children's Activity Center, where they can descend into a groundhog hole, climb a giant spiderweb, or invent an insect of their own design. Admission during July and August is $6.00 for adults and $3.00 for children. In May, June, September, and October the rate drops by half. Summer hours are daily 9:30 A.M. to 4:00 P.M.; spring and fall hours are the same on weekdays but 1:00 to 4:00 P.M. Saturdays and Sundays. For a calendar of the Science Center's many special events write P.O. Box 173, Holderness 03245; call (603) 968–7194.

In 1904, the heir of the man who invented and manufactured the soda fountain built a brick summer home in Center Harbor overlooking Squam Lake and the Squam mountain range. Unlike many northern homes, it had wide hallways, huge windows, and other elements of southern architecture; it was a showplace, even in an area rich in opulent private estates. It passed from his family through several owners, including minor European royalty, and eventually became Belknap College, which failed in the mid-1970s.

In 1985 its present owners bought the property and immediately began to restore and refurnish it to its original style. The result is ✦ **Red Hill Inn,** a period-piece mansion that visitors would gladly pay admission to tour. The inn is both lodging and restaurant, and it does both equally well. Despite its Victorian air, the relaxed feeling of a vacation home is still strong. Guest rooms and suites are bright and airy, with spectacular views over lawns, gardens, and the estate's farmhouse and barns to Squam Lake and the mountains beyond. In the evenings from the front rooms, dining room, and terrace, you can watch the setting sun turn the sky and lake to gold, the lawn to a brighter green, and the facing mountainsides dark with long shadows.

The food will demand your attention, even with the view for competition. Begin with half of a giant Spanish onion filled with artichoke hearts and aged cheddar. The milk-fed veal, fork tender, is in a caper sauce with tiny spring potatoes, and young tender rabbit is served with a shallot brown sauce. Desserts change daily and are just as original: apricot pie, Kentucky High (with bourbon and chocolate), and two old-time Yankee specialties—Indian pudding and vinegar pie. That's one you won't have a chance to try anywhere else. Cappuccino and espresso are offered, along with a nice selection of teas. Prices are moderate.

The bar in the lounge is half of a wooden hulled Cris Craft one of the owners bought after an accident had ruined the other side. The entire inn is decorated with the owners' collections, including several groups of early cameras. In the summer, guests can hike to tiny secluded beaches on Squam's shores, where the bottom is sandy and the water shallow enough for children to splash in safety for quite a distance. Rates for rooms and suites in the inn and the adjacent farmhouse vary with size and location, from $75.00 to $145.00 including a country breakfast. Write Red Hill Inn, Box 99M, Center Harbor 03226; call (603) 279–7001 or (800) 5–REDHILL.

Winter visitors to the Squam area can enjoy cross-country skiing free of charge at the **Red Hill Ski Touring Center** on Route 25B in Center Harbor. Intermediate- and beginner-level trails lead along the hillside meadows, through the woods, and along the shores of the lake. Rental ski equipment is available at Red Hill Inn.

THE EASTERN WHITE MOUNTAINS

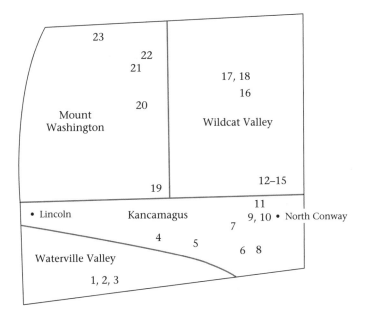

1. The Cascades
2. Welch-Dickey Mountain Trail
3. The Valley Inn
4. Sabbaday Falls
5. Rail 'n River Forest Trail
6. Indian Museum
7. Diana's Baths
8. Conway Scenic Railway
9. North Conway Depot
10. Mt. Washington Observatory Resource Center
11. Abenaki Encampment and Shop
12. Wentworth Resort
13. Jackson Falls
14. Jackson Ski Touring Foundation
15. The Inn at Thorn Hill
16. Glen Ellis Falls
17. Lost Pond
18. Crystal Cascade
19. Livermore
20. Mount Willard
21. Jefferson Notch
22. Cog Railway Museum
23. Zealand Falls

THE EASTERN WHITE MOUNTAINS

The White Mountains are the stuff of Indian legend and settlers' folk tales, of larger-than-life explorers and pioneers. Until the discovery of Crawford Notch, these mountains presented a barrier that kept the lands to the north in isolation.

In the nineteenth century they were "discovered" again, this time by wealthy families from the cities escaping the heat and dust. With maids, nannies, and enormous trunks, entire families boarded trains in New York, New Haven, Boston, Hartford, and other cities bound for Jackson, Glen, Twin Mountain, and Bretton Woods. Hotels sent elegant Concord Coaches, resplendent in canary yellow or cherry red with gold-leaf scrollwork, to welcome guests. They stayed all summer, hiking, riding, swimming (called "bathing"), playing lawn sports, and dancing to a full orchestra every evening. This annual social season lasted until World War II and the invention of air conditioning. Now most of the grand hotels are gone, but the few that remain have retained the fine traditions that made them famous in their golden age.

WATERVILLE VALLEY

Waterville Valley is a cul-de-sac cut deep into the White Mountain National Forest. Route 49 follows the Mad River, which is really quite benign except in the spring when it carries the runoff from a vast watershed and pours it into the Pemigewasset River. After 12 miles of narrow wooded passage, the valley opens suddenly into a broad floor of fields and a resort village reminiscent of an Alpine ski town.

Best known for its ski area, with the most ski terrain and lifts of any in New Hampshire, Waterville is also a favorite of families who feel perfectly safe letting their children travel between slopes and lodging in this isolated and hometown atmosphere. Its children's ski school has an area all of its own and is considered one of the nation's best places for children to learn to ski. Although Waterville has the atmosphere of a small resort, its facilities are state of the art and waits for lifts up Mount Tecumseh are rare indeed. Cross-country trails, sleigh rides through the White Mountain–ringed landscape, and an indoor skating rink complete the winter activities.

Waterville also includes 22 miles of hiking trails and several mountain summits whose trails begin in the valley. One of the shorter trails for more casual hiking begins at the bottom of the Snow's Mountain ski lift and leads to ◆ **The Cascades.** Follow the signs, climbing up the ski slope and then to the left. Be sure that you are following the sign for the Cascades trail and *not* the Snow's Mountain cross-country ski trail. Once you are in the woods, look for yellow trail blazes. There are very few steep places on this easy trail. Once you get to the cascades, cross the brook and continue up the other side for the best views of the continuous series of waterfalls and pools.

A pleasant, if moderately-difficult hike, ◆ **The Welch-Dickey Mountain Trail** combines views and natural history with a touch of mystery. To reach the trailhead parking area, take Upper Mad River Road, near the Thornton town line, then follow signs at the third junction to the right. Two trails begin here, joined into a loop that connects the two small mountains; the easier route begins with the right-hand trail toward Welch Mountain. Much of the trail is in the open, across ledges that give good views to the south and east. Before reaching the summit of Welch Mountain, the trail passes several stands of Jack Pine, exceedingly rare in New Hampshire. On Dickey Mountain, look for a cairn marking a stone circle carved into the bedrock. The origin of the circle is unknown, but if you stand inside it and look back toward the large triangular rock, you are looking at the exact point of the sunrise at the summer solstice. The 4½-mile climb takes about three-and-a-half hours.

For an outstanding dinner, reserve a table at ◆ **The Valley Inn,** where there is not a dull offering on the menu. The chef's signature entrée is a noisette of veal lightly breaded in crushed hazelnuts and served with an apple cream sauce, but the venison sautéed with wild mushrooms and port is just as tempting. Don't overlook the bread basket here. For reservations call (603) 236–8336.

OK, we admit it: We like the trappings of luxury, and our favorite place to stay in the valley is **The Snowy Owl.** Summer or winter, its three-story-tall fieldstone fireplace identifies it as a ski lodge. In the big downstairs lounge area, a sunken pit provides guests a place to gather by the fire in the evening. In the afternoon, wine and cheese await returning hikers and skiers.

Rooms are spacious; especially nice are the upper-level rooms with loft bunks for the kids. In-suite whirlpool baths, an indoor swimming pool, and a kids-stay-free policy make this contemporary inn an old-fashioned value. Families who prefer to do their own cooking will be happy at the **Black Bear Lodge,** where two-room suites sleep six and include kitchens stocked with cooking and eating utensils. Call (603) 236–8383 or (800) 258–8988 for information and reservations, and be sure to ask about their money-saving seasonal packages.

Except in winter, when the road is closed, a nice alternative route out of the valley is over **Thornton Gap,** a small notch reached from a road to the left at the village library. Follow signs to Tripoli (pronounced "triple-eye") Road, following a mountain brook through the forest.

After you crest the gap, you drop down into the Pemigewasset valley near **Russell Pond Campground.** For those who enjoy camping as a sport, not simply as a way to reduce lodging costs, this National Forest campground offers well-separated sites, deep in a hardwood forest that drops into a lovely small pond. No buildings mar its shore; there are a canoe launch, a fisherman or two, and the deep quiet that only lakes that ban motor boats can offer. There are no showers at the campground and no RV hookups. It's hard to believe that such quiet wilderness can be so close to an interstate highway.

THE KANCAMAGUS

Only one road cuts directly east and west through the center section of the White Mountain National Forest—the Kancamagus Highway. Not really a highway, but a paved two-lane road, it climbs from Lincoln to Conway over the 2,860-foot Kancamagus Pass via a long switchback. Be sure to stop at the pull-out areas to enjoy the view back across the mountains. No commercial development mars this route; you'll just find the woods, the views, small trailhead parking areas, and a handful of National Forest campgrounds.

At the eastern end, watch the south side of the road for the sign for ◈**Sabbaday Falls.** From the picnic area, the path is broad, smooth, and quite well marked to the foot of a flume, where the river flows through a 10-foot gap between straight rock walls more than 40 feet high. At the base there is a water-worn pothole about 4 feet in diameter, and nearby a 2-foot-wide stripe of dark basalt runs through the granite shelf that forms the viewing platform.

The trail along the rim is secured by a log railing, so you can safely look straight down into the flume. Full-grown trees cling to the opposite wall, their roots like giant fingers gripping the rock. You can see here very clearly the dramatic upstream march of the vertical wall of a waterfall. As potholes are formed by whirlpools, their walls are washed or worn away and the ledges are undercut.

About 3 miles east of the Sabbaday Falls trailhead is the Russell-Colbath house. This 1805 farmhouse has been restored to the mid-nineteenth century, providing an interesting look at the isolated lives of the families who settled the Passaconaway Valley. The house is open daily 9:00 A.M. to 4:30 P.M. between mid-June and Labor Day and on weekends after Memorial Day and until Columbus Day.

Behind the house, ❖ **Rail 'n River Forest Trail** is a half-mile, level loop that offers a unique view of the logging that once took place here and of the regrowth of the forest. Signboards and a free leaflet explain different kinds of forest environments, how timber was carried out of the valley by rail, and methods used to fight forest fires. The tale of the timbering that once stripped this entire area of its forests is now told only by ghosts, such as the pilings of a railroad bridge in the bed of the Swift River, visible from this trail. For a closer look at these rough-and-tumble days read *Tall Trees, Tough Men* by Robert E. Pike. The trail is wheelchair accessible.

Before the town of Conway and busy Route 16 you will reach Baldy's. This single building houses a small grocery store, a snowshoe shop, and an ❖ **Indian Museum.** The last two are the reason for our stop. Treffle Bolduc (Baldy) lived with the northern tribes and learned snowshoe making from them. You'll find his snowshoes all over northern New Hampshire, not only because they last, but because his prices are so reasonable that you can afford to outfit the whole family with snowshoes. Indian lore has been a lifetime interest for Baldy, and his collection of artifacts includes stone projectiles, baskets, cornhusk masks, snowshoes, quill baskets, birchbark containers, beaded mukluks, soapstone carving, and a birchbark canoe. This is not a fancy museum, but rather a collector's treasure trove, displayed in two small rooms with about as much light as the inside of a tepee. But it's real and reflects one man's zeal to preserve and treasure a way of life that very few people have shared. Admission is $5.00 for adults, $2.00 for children; the museum is open daily from 2:00 to 5:00 P.M., except in the winter, when it closes at 4:00 P.M. The store is open longer hours, into the evening in the summer, so someone will probably let you into the museum at times other than its official hours. Call (603) 447–5287 for information.

Route 16 from the northern end of Conway to above North Conway is so beaten a path that on summer and fall weekends the traffic may be backed up for hours. But there is a way around it, and it takes you past two delightful corners that people honking their horns on Route 16 never hear about. But first you have to find West Side Road. Just opposite the intersection where Route 153 heads south to Eaton Center is a street going north. Take it and then the left at the fork (straight ahead is one of Conway's **covered bridges,** and to the left you will pass another one just a few yards up the road). Follow this road through lovely farmlands that open out to some of the valley's finest views of the Presidential Range.

When the road comes to a T, you should go left to bypass North Conway, or right to reach the ski area or the northern edge, above the outlets.

Less than a mile to the north, on the left of West Side Road, is the unmarked trailhead to ◆**Diana's Baths.** Look for a wide, straight, gravel road, between two fenced fields, which ends abruptly at the edge of the woods. Only here will you finally find the signs identifying the trail.

The falls, only ½ mile along a fairly level trail, were once the site of a gristmill. You can still see the foundations and the chute that fed it water. Above, falls and pools are interspersed with cascades over sloping granite. Each of these succeeding shelves is marked by potholes cut into its surface, like a series of children's marble holes on a playground. As you continue to climb, you will find the ledges flatten and the falls shorten. But the swirls and scoops in the granite become even more dramatic.

Another way of getting to North Conway without encountering the outlet traffic, is to ride the ◆**Conway Scenic Railway** from the quieter town of Conway. The tracks cut through the peaceful, historic heart of the valley, passing fields, meadows, woodlands, the Saco River, and an abandoned lumber mill. The Presidential Range fills the north end of the valley and dramatic ledges line the west. Or, if you begin the trip in North Conway, you can enjoy a good lunch en route in the dining car, a period piece in honey-colored wood and etched glass. Trains run daily from mid-May through foliage season, weekends as early as April and as late as September, but in order to ride from Conway and have any time in North Conway, you have to ride between May and October when there are multiple trains each day. Write to the railway at P.O. Box 1947, North Conway 03860; telephone (603) 356–5251 or (800) 232–5251.

You don't have to ride the train to enjoy the museum at the ◈**North Conway Depot,** a beautifully restored Victorian railway station in the center of town at the northern terminus of the trip. Displayed in the old waiting room are brochures, lanterns, uniforms, photos, and other historical items. Be sure to ask for the flyer identifying the buildings, railway cars, and engines in the rail yard. Many of the cabooses are private homes; other cars and engines are in the process of restoration. Telephone (603) 356–5251.

Before the return ride to Conway, walk across the wide town green to **Zebs General Store,** which carries only products made in New England. Look for fine foods from small farms and bakeries, unique handmade items, books, soaps, and an array of other items you won't find elsewhere.

The ◈**Mt. Washington Observatory Resource Center,** on Route 16 in North Conway, is a good stop if you can't make it to the summit of Mt. Washington. The center has exhibits on the history and work of the observatory, the Summit Road, the Cog Railway, the mountain hotels, and local hiking. Students of the mountains will find the center's collection of rare books, magazines, and pamphlets an invaluable resource. Exhibits are open daily 9:00 A.M. to 5:00 P.M., May 15 to October 15; the library is open Thursdays only. Write them at P.O. Box 2310, North Conway 03860; telephone (603) 356–8345.

In Intervale, back on Route 16, is a scenic overlook with a fine panorama of the mountains and Cathedral Ledge. Opposite is Intervale Crossroad, right beside the post office. Only about 100 yards up this road on your left, you will see a little cabin and a stone with a bronze plaque. Park and cross the railroad to the

◆ **Abenaki Encampment and Shop.** Each summer, from 1884 until 1964, members of the Abenaki tribe came from their winter home in Quebec to Cathedral Woods, where they camped and traded with guests of the White Mountain hotels, who visited the encampment to watch the Abenaki weave baskets, which made fine souvenirs. Stephen Laurent, son of the Abenaki chief who started the encampment, still owns the property and the little shop that has been in use there since the late nineteenth century.

Go when you can spend some time to hear the stories of this Abenaki scholar, who is continuing his father's life work of writing a dictionary of the Abenaki language. Along with sweetgrass baskets, beadwork, and Nemadji earth pottery, there are publications on Indian culture for sale. An authentic birchbark wigwam stands nearby under majestic pine trees. The shop, which is listed on the National Register of Historic Places, is open daily from June 15 to October 15, 10:00 A.M. to noon and 3:00 to 5:00 P.M.

Running parallel to often-busy Route 16 through Intervale is Route 16A, which was bypassed by the new road. Now a quiet residential byway, the road was once lined with inns and hotels. A few remain, among them **The Forest,** which has hosted travelers continuously since it opened in 1890. Today its rooms are furnished in lovingly restored antiques; rooms on the top floor have recessed windows set inside the slope of the mansard roof. It's the kind of inn where guests gather in the evening to share experiences with the lively innkeepers. Perhaps the spirit of the place is best described in the attitude of this hospitable couple: "Spending time with our guests is what makes this business fun." Groomed cross-country ski trails begin at the door and downhill skiing is minutes away. Don't plan an early start, however, since breakfast is well worth lingering over. The Forest is part of **"Bike the Whites"** and a similar cross-country ski package with two other inns (See p. 87). Write to The Forest at P.O. Box 37, Intervale 03845; telephone (800) 448–3534.

WILDCAT VALLEY

Tucked into a corner, away from the hustle to the south, is the village of Jackson, with its red covered bridge and white church. Artists discovered its scenic beauty in the mid-1800s, and by the turn of the century, Jackson had twenty-four lodging places,

Abenaki Encampment

including several grand hotels. By the late 1970s, only Eagle Mountain House and a few smaller guest houses were still operating.

But this story has a happier ending than most. Today a number of these have reopened, including the Victorian treasure, Wentworth Hall. Not all of its original thirty-nine buildings could be saved from years of neglect and abandonment, but the three central ones and several other cottages with their curved porches, round towers, wide gables, and quirky architectural detail are once again the showpiece of the village center.

The ◆**Wentworth Resort** is just as nice inside as it is outside, with real feather pillows, giant bathtubs, and an air of grandeur that is comfortable, not intimidating. Rooms in the Arden, Wildwood, and Amster cottages are unique, taking advantage of the architecture of each. In the main building, the Thornycroft suite is our favorite, with its carefully restored antiques, custom-built bed, window seat, and sleigh settee, its marble fireplace, and even a fireplace in the ample Jacuzzi room.

The dining room is just as memorable; the menu is innovative, but not just for the sake of being different. Each season brings new dishes as the chef takes advantage of the freshest ingredients. Smoked duck breast may be served on a bed of grilled red onions, onion soup laced with cider and cheddar, veal topped with morels and brandy, or quail stuffed with wild rice and cashews, as we would expect from a chef with such a careful eye to detail. The public is invited to dine here but should call to make reservations. The hotel is open year-round. Write the Wentworth Resort Hotel, Box M, Jackson 03846; call (603) 383–9700 or (800) 637–0013.

A short walk up the road is ◆**Jackson Falls,** a series of cascades with potholes that invite jumping into, if the weather is only halfway nice. The hotel has a pool, of course, but these falls must have been the original inspiration for water slides. There is a circular route of 6 miles (called, for some reason, the Five Mile Drive) that begins at the Wentworth and goes up the Carter Notch Road past the falls. Instead of continuing to the top of the notch (where the road turns into a trail), turn right and cross the river for views across highland meadows to the mountains.

Black Mountain Ski Area is usually forgotten in the razzmatazz of its bigger neighbors, but this end-of-the-road place is a favorite of anyone who has ever skied there. Skiing on Black

Mountain has been synonymous with **Whitney's** since "Ma" Whitney bought the old Moody Farm in 1936 and welcomed skiers to the first overhead ski lift in the East on Black Mountain, literally out her back door. The lift was made from Sears Roebuck shovel handles. Generations of skiers later, **Whitney's Inn Jackson** still welcomes skiers, Black Mountain has grown into a full-service ski area whose lift rates are one of the best ski values in the White Mountains, and "Ma" Whitney has retired to a house on the edge of the slopes above the inn. Comfortable rooms, a hearty breakfast, and special facilities and programs for children make Whitney's popular with families. It's a year-round resort as well, with special summer packages that include a Wednesday night lobster cookout. Whitney's address is Post Office Box W, Route 16B, Jackson 03846; telephone (603) 383–8916 or (800) 677–5737.

Cross-country skiing is an art form in Jackson. This is the home of the ◈**Jackson Ski Touring Foundation,** which maintains 150 kilometers of exceptionally well-groomed trails throughout the village and all over the surrounding hillsides. In winter, with no leaves to obscure the view, the neighboring mountains, including the southern slopes of Mount Washington, are visible from every hillside. It's so beautiful on a crisp winter day that it's hard to concentrate on skiing.

Just high enough above the center of Jackson Village to give it a full view of Mt. Washington, ◈**The Inn at Thorn Hill** was designed by Stanford White and built in 1895. Its Victorian legacy is nicely preserved; guest rooms are individually decorated, although the views from nearly every window would be decoration enough. Like Sugar Hill in the western White Mountains, Jackson is a small town that looms large on the culinary map, and the inn's outstanding dining room eclipses even the views. Rarely have we been offered a selection so difficult to choose from—a galette of smoked tomato, pancetta, basil, and parmesan and a smoked trout and grilled pear salad were two of the starter selections we ordered before we even reached the entrées. Four-course dinners are included in the room rate, or served to nonguests at a fixed price of $28. Along with direct access to the network of cross-country trails and proximity to four ski areas, the inn offers tobogganing on the property, even at night. Art and photography workshops with artists from Cape Ann are a long-standing tradition at the inn, which can be reached at Thorn Hill Road, Post Office Box A, Jackson Village 03846; telephone (603) 383–4242 or (800) 289–8990.

Near the top of Pinkham Notch on Route 16 is a trio of short, rewarding hikes. Look for the parking area for ◆**Glen Ellis Falls** on the west side of the road. This short walk, beginning at the tunnel under the highway, leads to the cliff-lined Ellis River, which plunges over cascades and then through a narrow cleft in the granite, falling 65 feet into a basin before continuing through its boulder-strewn bed.

The Appalachian Mountain Club Visitor Center, just up the road, is the starting point for the ½-mile walk to ◆**Lost Pond.** Cross Route 16 to the east side. The trail crosses a bridge then runs south for ½-mile to the pond. While the falls shows the wild side of nature, this shallow pond shows a gentler, more tranquil wilderness. At the southern end is a beaver dam and a jumble of boulders, dropped here from the slopes above. In dry weather the path continues on to Glen Ellis Falls.

◆**Crystal Cascade** is an easy fifteen-minute walk up the trail behind the Visitor Center, following the Cutler River upstream. Although called a cascade, this is really a falls, the water dropping almost vertically 60 feet into a deep chasm and then falling another 20 feet. We have always felt that the best place to view a waterfall is facing its midpoint, a vantage usually reserved for winged creatures. But the unique bend in the river provides an overlook at exactly the right point for viewing this one.

MOUNT WASHINGTON

At just over a mile high, Mount Washington is the highest mountain in the northeast, but its weather conditions are among the most severe in the world. Arctic equipment is tested at its summit. Only sightly below it stand other mountains named for presidents—thus the name "Presidential Range."

Crawford Notch, a break in the almost solid chain of the White Mountains, lies due south of Mount Washington. Geologically, the notch is a classic glacial scour. During the Ice Age, boulders frozen into the ice caught onto chunks of loose bedrock as the glacier moved down mountain slopes. In valleys, where the action of the glacier became more concentrated, the scouring was at its greatest, carrying off boulders and pieces of broken cliffs which in turn scraped even deeper as they moved, giving a characteristic U-shaped curve to the valley walls.

In the early days of settlement, vast forests of very tall trees covered all but the tops of the mountains, so the settlers couldn't tell where the notches and the passes were. About all they could do was follow the riverbeds, hoping to find the easiest and lowest route.

Usually, these routes were discovered more or less by accident. So it was with Timothy Nash the day he climbed a tree on Cherry Mountain while moose hunting and saw the gap in the line of mountains. He went to Portsmouth to ask the royal governor (the same Benning Wentworth we met earlier) for a piece of land and a road through the notch. The governor told him to bring a horse through the notch, which Timothy and a friend did by lowering it over the cliff on a rope. Nash got his land, and eventually the road was built, opening a much shorter route to the north country.

The trees that filled the notch, like those of the Passaconaway Valley, fell to the lumber market. Entire towns sprang up around the lumber camps, and some of them died with the industry. ♦**Livermore,** a ghost town today, lies along Sawyer River Road, which meets Route 302 just north of the bridge over the Sawyer River about 5 miles north of Bartlett. A mile and a half up Sawyer River Road you'll see a barred gate and some foundations, which are all that is left of Livermore. It was once a thriving community of 200, built in the late 1800s and reached by both road and railroad. Of its homes, stores, boarding houses, offices, and two saw mills, you'll find only ruins. Walk to the river and into the woods upstream to find cellar holes and the ruins of a beautifully constructed concrete and brick sawmill. All of these have full-sized trees growing out of them now. It's easier to find the cellar holes in the fall when the leaves are missing. Look for the one with the company safe clearly visible.

Just north of the Sawyer River Road is the **Notchland Inn,** a granite mansion that has been a Crawford Notch landmark since its construction in 1862. The front parlor of this Victorian home was designed by Gustav Stickley; an adjoining country schoolhouse has been transformed into two suites. Guests can join a guided walk to a dramatic gorge and swimming hole located on the property or, in winter, go for a sleigh ride. The Notchland

Inn is on Route 302, Harts Location 03812; call (603) 374–6131 or (800) 866–6131.

At the "head" of the notch is a narrow gateway and the **old train station** where the summer guests arrived, bound for the Crawford House Hotel, which once stood guard over the notch. The hotel is gone, but the little Victorian station is an Appalachian Mountain Club (AMC) information center, where you can get trail maps and advice if you plan to do any serious climbing.

The best view of Crawford Notch is down into it from ◆**Mount Willard,** an easy climb (more accurately, an uphill walk) along an old bridle path to the summit. From there you can see the great scoop of the notch below you, as well as the shimmering cascades that fall off the mountains through rocky ravines. Watch overhead for peregrine falcons, which have nesting sites near the summit of Mount Willard.

Past Saco Lake, which is the source of the Saco River, is Mount Clinton Road, which leads to ◆**Jefferson Notch.** Possibly the least known of the White Mountain notches, its 3,009-foot elevation is the highest point in the state reached by a public road. Gravel all the way, the road passes through deep woods along Monroe Brook, which cascades over rocks between moss-covered banks. At the top, the forest is still too tall to allow any panoramic views, but drive into the parking lot for a good, close view of Mount Washington's summit, 3,000 feet above you. The road descends into the town of Jefferson; the entire trip is 9 miles.

While the Cog Railway to the summit of Mount Washington is one of the state's best known attractions, the new ◆**Cog Railway Museum** at the base station enjoys less celebrity. Located opposite the ticket window on the ground floor, its displays include cutaway versions of an early coach and boiler, showing how these were originally built and how they worked. There are also exhibits on the mountain's unusual weather, the history of the railway, and other related subjects. There is an admission charge, except for those who hold tickets for the train. The museum is open daily May through October. Telephone (603) 846–5404 or (800) 922–8825, ext. 5.

While the **Mount Washington Hotel** is a White Mountain landmark, few know the **Bretton Arms,** a former chauffeur's quarters that served as home to the Secretariat during the Bretton Woods Monetary Conference in 1944. Now an inn and a National

Stables at Bretton Arms

Historic Landmark, the Bretton Arms offers newly-renovated guest rooms and a more intimate atmosphere than the grand hotel up the hill. Be sure to see the magnificent Victorian stable building just past the inn, where horses, sleighs, and carriages are still housed. The Bretton Arms is located next to the cross-country ski center at Bretton Woods 03575; telephone (603) 278–1000 or (800) 258–0330.

Instead of leaving the area via Jefferson Notch, you can continue along Route 302 to the Zealand Campground, where there is
a nice picnic area along the Ammonoosuc River. If you continue
up the Zealand Road, about 3½ miles to its end, you can take the
Zealand Trail to ◆ **Zealand Falls,** a 2½-mile, easy hike. Getting
to the top of the falls is the only climbing involved—there is only
about a 350-foot difference in altitude from the parking lot to the
top of the falls. The falls is really a cascade, and at its top, from the
AMC hut, is a view of New Hampshire's hidden notch. Only hikers
can see the dramatic shape of Zealand Notch, for no road pene-
trates it at any point. Take a lunch to eat by the falls as you enjoy
the view. Along the trail you will follow the bed of a nineteenth-
century logging railroad and pass through hardwood forests. It's
hard to picture this entire valley laid waste by uncontrolled lum-
bering and the resulting fire and erosion damage, so great was
the ability of the forest to rejuvenate itself here.

About halfway up the Zealand Road is the **Sugarloaf Campground,** one of the loveliest and most secluded in the mountains. Roomy sites are carved out of young forest, some with direct
paths to the rocky Zealand River below. Resident hosts, a lively
couple who have camped here for more than thirty years, occupy
a central campsite all summer and can tell you where the best
fishing and blueberrying are. For information, write to the District
Ranger, White Mountain National Forest, Bethlehem 03574.

THE WESTERN
WHITE MOUNTAINS

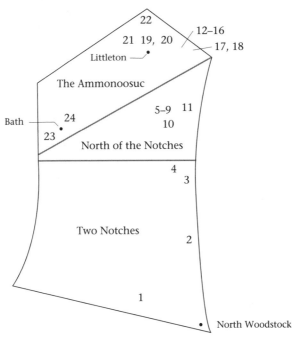

22

21 19, 20

12–16

17, 18

Littleton

The Ammonoosuc

Bath

24

5–9   11

10

23

North of the Notches

4

3

Two Notches

2

1

North Woodstock

1. Kinsman Notch
2. Cascade Brook and
   Kinsman Falls
3. New England Ski Museum
4. The Rim Trail
5. Harman's Store
6. Sugar Hill Historical Museum
7. Hilltop Inn
8. North Country Chamber
   Players
9. Sunset Hill House
10. Franconia iron furnace
11. Robert Frost Place

12. The Rocks
13. Bretzfelder Memorial Park
14. Gepetto's Barn
15. Adair
16. Tim-Bir Alley Restaurant
17. Maplewood
18. Newt Washburn
19. Wallace Horse Cemetery
20. Littleton Historical Museum
21. Kilburn Crags
22. Moore Station Dam
23. Bath Village Bridge
24. Upper Village

THE WESTERN WHITE MOUNTAINS

The summer social season on this side of the White Mountains involved not only guests at the grand hotels—Profile House, Forest Hills, Sunset Hill, and the resorts of Bethlehem—but an increasing number of wealthy people who built their own summer estates, especially in Sugar Hill and Bethlehem. When the era of hotel summers ended, these families continued to return. Some retired here, giving the area a permanent cultural tradition that shows today in regular art and music events.

This land is beautiful and the mountains a little less craggy than the Presidential Range to the east. Towns here have less of a seasonal air about them, being year-round communities with their own economic base. Downtown stores cater more to local needs than to tour-bus shopping expeditions. Hospitality is warm, and visitors return to the same inn year after year.

Country stores, covered bridges, farms, and mountain streams punctuate the miles of forests bordering the winding country roads. Only the stone walls that wind through the woodlands remind us that much of this land was once cleared for farming. This is a place for relaxing, exploring, and savoring.

TWO NOTCHES

The White Mountain National Forest's westernmost segment begins just south of Sugar Hill and Franconia. Route 116 continues past the Frost Place to the town of Easton, high in the hills and completely surrounded by the national forest. South of Easton on Route 112 is a wild and beautiful notch almost completely overshadowed by the fame of neighboring Franconia Notch.

The road through ◆ **Kinsman Notch** winds and curves and climbs until it reaches tiny Beaver Lake, a high mountain tarn, rockbound and icy cold. In its center rises a rocky, pine-clad island. The landscape here is wild and almost desolate under the slope of Mount Blue—but nowhere near as forbidding as it must have looked to Asa Kinsman and his wife. With their household goods on a two-wheeled cart pulled by oxen, they discovered that they had taken the wrong track to their new home in Landaff. Instead of turning back to go around the mountains that lay in their way, they hacked a path through the notch. If you take a turn you didn't plan on or miss the road you wanted, just remember the Kinsmans and take heart.

At its top the notch opens out, giving excellent views down the valley to the east. The narrowness and curves of the road at the top give a real sense of this being a pass, more so than some of the better-known notches. (You may notice that the state highway map has the Kinsman Notch label a little to the east of its actual location 6 miles from North Woodstock.)

Franconia Notch is one of the most frequently visited spots in New Hampshire, and it is the home of the state's symbol, The **Old Man of the Mountains.** It was to protect the fragile ledges of this famous stone profile from the dangers of blasting that Interstate 93 was stopped just below the notch and resumed just above it. It took a U.S. congressman with the courage to dig in his heels and take on the whole of Washington, but the integrity of the notch was saved, and its hidden treasures remain in seclusion despite the number of visitors at its famous attractions. A bicycle path runs the length of the notch, crossing the highway through specially-built underpasses.

A trail from the glacial formation known as the Basin leads to ✦ **Cascade Brook and Kinsman Falls.** Although these cascades are not ten minutes' level walk from the Basin, they are never crowded and provide a fine place to picnic or just explore. The ledges over which the brook slides and drops have been worn into graceful curves, potholes, tiny flumes, and gorges by the brook. In places the water spreads over the granite in a smooth sheet; elsewhere it falls in ribbons from pool to pool. You can climb through the woods along the trail or up the sloping face of the ledges. When water is high or the weather rainy, it's better to stay on the trail and avoid the slippery rocks.

At the head of the notch, by the base of the Aerial Tramway, is the ✦ **New England Ski Museum.** Permanent and changing exhibits tell the story of this sport with historical equipment, photographs, art, and even changing fashions in skiwear. Open daily December 26 to March 31, 11:00 A.M. to 4:00 P.M., and Memorial Day weekend to October 15, noon to 5:00 P.M.; the admission is free. Write The New England Ski Museum, P.O. Box 267, Franconia 03580; call (603) 823–7177.

✦ **The Rim Trail** can be reached from the top of the Aerial Tramway (look for one of its original 1930s cars at the Ski

Museum) or via the Kinsman Ridge trail from the head of Franconia Notch. It offers hikers panoramic views into the notch and across the Franconia and Presidential ranges along the exposed rim and from the observation tower at the end. Notice the scar on the steep facing slope of Mount Lafayette, caused by a 1959 landslide that covered the road through the notch with 27 feet of debris. Even today, the physical forces of weathering and erosion continue the work of the glaciers in changing the landscape of the notches. Be sure to watch for peregrine falcons that nest on Eagle Cliff, below, where golden eagles once laid their eggs.

NORTH OF THE NOTCHES

Over the hills, on Route 117, lies Sugar Hill, stretched along the top of a ridge overlooking some of the White Mountains' most beautiful scenery. It's the kind of genteel town where people wave to you from their front porches as you go for an evening walk. ◆**Harman's Store** should be your first stop, for fine aged cheddar that bears no resemblance to the grocery-store stuff. Harman's sends cheese and first-run New Hampshire maple syrup to people all over the country who don't really believe that there is a town named Sugar Hill. The secret of their cheese is that they buy fine cheddar and then age it themselves. You'll find New Hampshire jams and jellies, soldier beans, common crackers, and whole-wheat pancake flour here, too, and all grades of the New Hampshire maple syrup that gave Sugar Hill its name. They also sell Vermont syrup for those people who won't believe that maple trees grow all over New England, New York, and Quebec (but the proprietors snicker a little behind their counter when they do). Open year-round daily, May to October, closed Sundays November to April. Call Harman's Cheese and Country Store at (603) 823–8000.

Across the street is the ◆**Historical Museum.** Housed in three buildings, the exhibits show, through an exceptional collection of old photographs, artifacts, carriages, and furnishings, the daily life of early settlers and Sugar Hill's heyday as a summer resort. Here are the kitchen from a stagecoach tavern with its original furnishings, a blacksmith shop, the ornate wagon of a local hotel, and a genealogical library. Admission is only $2.00 ($1.00 for seniors and children ages twelve or older). Open from

Hilltop Inn

July 1 through late October, Thursday, Saturday, and Sunday, 1:00 to 4:00 P.M. (603–823–8142).

Within walking distance of both of these is ❖ **Hilltop Inn.** This is one of those places that friends hesitate to tell you about because they are afraid it will become so popular that there won't be room for them. The 1895 Victorian home is decorated with period furniture but offers every modern comfort. Big beds, plenty of pillows for late-night readers, flannel sheets, and antique linens are just a few of the luxuries. But the real charm of the Hilltop Inn is its owners, Meri and Mike Hern. Their offbeat sense of humor and irrepressible enthusiasm make old friends out of strangers from the first rumble of Mike's contagious chuckle. Guests had raved about Meri's breakfasts for so long that they are now open for dinner as well (by reservation). Write Hilltop Inn, Main Street, Sugar Hill 03585; call (603) 823–5695.

The menu changes weekly, and may include such delicacies as fresh spring fiddleheads, a delicately seasoned cassoulet, basil ravioli with smoked salmon, or artichoke bottoms filled with lobster. An extensive wine list, espresso, cappuccino, and sumptuous desserts round out a fine dinner. People travel some distance to eat here, so be sure to reserve early. The restaurant is open 6:00 to 8:00 P.M. Wednesday through Saturday from Memorial Day through October 31, Friday and Saturday in the winter. The Inn is open all year; rates are moderate.

Since its heyday as a summer resort, Sugar Hill has had a flourishing arts community and hosts the ◆**North Country Chamber Players** annual summer festival in the Meeting House on Friday evenings in July and August. Members of this organization hold first-chair positions in major orchestras. For a complete schedule of concerts write Box 99, Franconia 03580 or call (603) 869–3154.

The ◆**Sunset Hill House** was one of the grandest of the White Mountain resort hotels, on the crest of a hill with mountain views in all directions. A boardwalk connected it to the village so that ladies could stroll up to watch the sunset without soiling the hems of their gowns. The main building is gone now, but a second one dating from 1882 has just been restored to an opulence that made the original hotel famous. Guest rooms are beautiful and comfortable, with a view from every window. The dining room overlooks the Presidential Range, which on clear evenings is bathed in a rosy reflection of the sunset known as alpen-glow. Dinner guests may have trouble giving the menu the attention it deserves until after dusk claims the mountains, but the flavors of dishes such as chicken and spinach roulade, grilled shrimp with black bean cake, or wild mushroom ravioli with port sauce can compete with any view on equal terms. There is no off-season here, with sleigh rides, cross-country trails, golf, hiking, and maple sugaring available from the front door and ski slopes minutes away. Write Sunset Hill House, Sunset Hill Road, Sugar Hill 03585; telephone (603) 823–5522 or (800) SUNHILL.

In the valley of the Gale River, east of Sugar Hill, Franconia was once the center of an iron industry that thrived from 1811 until the 1850s. The ore came from mines close to Sunset Hill House; the vein was the richest then known. The giant stone **iron furnace** where ore was smelted still stands by the river, near the LaFayette Regional School. An interpretive center and outdoor panels explain the process that turned ore into wrought-iron bars. Inside the building, which is open irregular hours, is a scale model of the furnace, cut away to show its interior. This is the only iron furnace remaining in the state.

South of the village, off Route 116, the ❖**Robert Frost Place** is a small weathered farmhouse, its mailbox marked R. FROST. Along with Robert Frost memorabilia and autographed first editions, there are a slide show, a nature trail marked with lines of his poetry, and a rare collection of the poet's less-known work: Christmas card verses. Open Saturday and Sunday 1:00 to 5:00 P.M. Memorial Day through June 30 and every afternoon except Tuesday from July 1 until Columbus Day. The Frost Place is in Franconia; call (603) 823–5510.

Although nothing remains of the Forest Hills, another of the grand resort hotels, one of its "cottages" has been restored and is again welcoming guests. **The Inn at Forest Hills** has eight guest rooms, each furnished in a highly individual style. The walls of the sun-filled Daniel Webster room, for example, are decorated in framed antique fashion prints. Breakfast is an event here, with menus changing daily. Guests have free access to a local cross-country ski network; hiking, bicycling, and downhill ski trails are minutes away. Prices are moderate. For reservations, write to P.O. Box 783, Franconia 03580, or call (603) 823–9550 or (800) 280–9550; fax (603) 823–8701.

THE AMMONOOSUC

Bethlehem, now a quiet town stretched out along a ridge, was once a major resort capital of the White Mountains. Along its main street stood thirty of the biggest and the grandest hotels, a summer-long procession of splendor and gaiety. They are gone now, but the elegant cottages that surrounded them are still there—some serving today as bed and breakfasts—and so is the pure pollen-free mountain air that attracted the first visitors.

Its quiet streets and airy location make Bethlehem a good base for exploring the national forest, where the ban on commercial activity leaves no lodging for those who don't enjoy camping. **The Mulburn Inn** is a bed and breakfast in the Ivie Estate built for the heiress of the Woolworth fortune. The woodwork of maple, mahogany, oak, and ash is in mint condition, and a

117

round sitting room (even the window glass is curved) forms the base of one of the inn's towers. Rooms are beautifully furnished and unique—one has its original raspberry-pink art deco bathroom fixtures, and another has the town's only elevator for a closet. Write the inn at Main Street, Bethlehem 03574; call (603) 869–3389. Just down Main Street from the Mulburn Inn is **Rosa Flamingo's,** a contemporary restaurant known for its pizza and varied lunch and dinner menu. Call (603) 869–3111.

There are, it is said, more architectural styles in Bethlehem than in any other New England town. It's easy to believe. But the most unusual must be **The Bells,** a pagoda-shaped three-story cottage on Strawberry Hill Street. For a self-guided tour that reveals some of Bethlehem's lively architectural and social heritage, get a copy of the booklet "An Illustrated Tour of Bethlehem," sold locally for $2.00.

Next to the neoclassical Methodist Church on Main Street is the outlet store for **Nanook Children's Wear.** You've seen these clothes in boutiques and fashionable catalogs, but you've probably never seen them at these prices. Look for the boxes, where you can pull out eyelet party dresses or whatever they have too many of that week. This is a good place to stock up for Christmas. Nanook Children's Wear is on Main Street in Bethlehem (603–869–5761).

◆ **The Rocks,** west of Bethlehem on Route 302, a late nineteenth-century farm estate, is now in the care of the Society for the Protection of New Hampshire Forests. The double-stone walls, the buttresses, and the lower story of the Victorian barn were built of stones cleared from the rolling pastures and meadows that surround the house and barns. A free leaflet describes the sights along a 2-mile self-guided trail past a highly original sawmill-pigpen and a bee house, and through forest and wetlands.

Another self-guided trail, through the Christmas tree plantations, describes the growing of trees and some of the estate's history, as it leads to a scenic overview.

Seasonal activities are planned on weekends year-round, with a Halloween festival, hay-wagon tours of the Christmas tree plantation (along with cut-your-own sales), a winter forest festival with logging demonstrations, snowshoe tours, maple sugaring, and a wildflower festival. Nature trails and gardens are free and always open; there are fees for special programs, and registration is necessary for some. Write Society for the Protection of New Hampshire Forests, The Rocks, RFD #1, Bethlehem 03574; call (603) 444–6228.

Off Prospect Street and also managed by the same society is the ◆**Bretzfelder Memorial Park,** seventy-seven acres of forest, pond, mountain brook, and picnic area connected by walking and cross-country trails. A leaflet tells about the various trees and signs along the trails explain the natural history and ecology. The story of Mr. Bretzfelder and his favorite tree (the tree is still alive even after major surgery) is told on a sign by the entrance. On Wednesday evenings in July and August at 8:00 P.M., the Evening Rambles explore some aspect of the park—its nocturnal animals, wildflowers, or other subject. No admission is charged; call (603) 444–6228 for dates and a description of the programs.

Just east of the entrance to The Rocks on Route 302, Brook Road leads to Blaney Road, on which stands ◆**Gepetto's Barn,** the workshop of Win Brebner. There he creates toys, furniture, puzzles, castles, chests of blocks, and other useful things of wood. The prices are even more surprising—a good-sized toy box filled with blocks is $50. Doll furniture runs about $3.00. There's no telling what you'll find here; you just have to go and look around. Gepetto's Barn, Blaney Road, Bethlehem 03574, is open Memorial Day weekend to Columbus Day weekend, from morning until dusk. Call (603) 444–2187.

◆**Adair,** built in 1927 by Washington D.C. lawyer Frank Hogan, illustrates the popularity of Bethlehem as a summer resort into this century. Family occupied until 1991, this gracious home, set on grounds landscaped by Frederick Law Olmsted, has hosted presidents, Supreme Court justices, and other celebrities. Its new owners have made Adair into an exceptional inn, with elegance, comfort, and noticeable warmth. Original artwork decorates the eight tasteful guest rooms. Spacious parlors and the gardens and lawns of the estate create an atmosphere designed for relaxation. A stay here is well worth the higher-than-average rates. A full breakfast includes several house specialties.

Adair has lured Tim and Biruta Carr, owners of ◆**Tim-Bir Alley** restaurant, to move into the inn's two elegant dining rooms. Formerly in Littleton, Tim-Bir Alley provides an exceptional dining experience. The menu changes daily, featuring at least three entrées, and might start with grilled eggplant and

119

warm goat cheese on roasted red pepper coulis, followed by an entrée of duck breast with fig-almond chutney on pear purée or salmon with fresh basil and garlic-infused olive oil. Local residents would like to keep this restaurant their own secret. Adair and Tim-Bir Alley are off Route 302, just west of the Rocks Estate, on Old Littleton Road, Bethlehem 03574; telephone (603) 444–2600 (fax 444–4823).

◆**Maplewood** was not just the largest and grandest of the local hotels; it was a village of its own with Victorian railroad station, farms to provide food for its dining rooms, a sugar bush that yielded one hundred gallons of syrup each spring, a golf course, and a casino with a ballroom, movie theater, and full bowling alley. The hotel is gone, but the village of Maplewood is still on the map. The restored casino with its stone tower still guards the golf course and four wonderful old "cottages"—great hulking things with porches and gabled windows—are situated in a row just east of the casino.

Beyond them is a little shrine by the side of the road with a lovely story to tell. From the beginning of the century until 1949, underprivileged boys from a Boston industrial school were brought up in the summers to work as caddies at Maplewood. In 1958, a number of the former caddies, many of them prominent and successful, built the shrine. To this day these men gather at Maplewood for reunions.

Not far from Bethlehem, on its way to Whitefield, Route 142 drops down a long steep hill. At the very bottom, just as the road curves to the left, is the tiny brown workshop of a man who has been honored by the President and whose work is on permanent display at The Smithsonian Institution. ◆**Newt Washburn** is a fourth-generation Abenaki basketmaker, one of fewer than half a dozen who have continued in this art. He designs and makes his own tools, the knives and splitters with which he turns an ash log into a finely woven basket. On a full-sized basket each splint is the thickness of a growth ring separated from the log, but for smaller ones Newt splits each one in half to keep its thickness in proportion to the its width. Newt will show you the whole process, from log to basket, and his scrapbook too. Museum-quality Abenaki baskets run from $55 to $100, a real bargain for an original by a craftsman of his reputation. Newt Washburn's workshop is in Bethlehem Hollow (603–869–5894).

Arriving in Littleton on Route 302, **Bishop's Homemade Ice Cream Shoppe** is in a white house on the right. If you can think of any excuse to stop and try this ice cream, do it. You can sit at picnic tables on the lawn or inside the upbeat green-and-white ice cream parlor while you enjoy the old favorite flavors, a wide variety of homemade yogurt flavors, or one of their unique recipes. For calorie watchers or those with cholesterol problems, there are sorbets rich with the taste of real fruit. The Bishop's Bash is filled with chunks of brownie, walnuts, and chocolate chips, and their brandy Alexander ice cream "is as close to the real thing that we serve at our New Year's Eve party as we can get without a liquor license," the owner explains. Open daily from mid-April until mid-October at 78 Cottage Street in Littleton; call (603) 444–6039.

Opposite Bishop's, Mt. Eustice Road travels under Interstate 93, just beyond which a short lane leads to the ◆**Wallace Horse Cemetery.** Inside a small corral are three graves and a family stone; on the fence a placard explains the touching story of the team of matched bay Morgans, buried here with all their regalia, that were the only "children" of the Wallaces from 1889 until the death of the horses in 1919. As touching as the story recounted here are the pennies that visitors have placed on the stones.

Throughout northern New Hampshire you will see photographs of the White Mountains "the way we were" during the Golden Age. Most of these were reproduced from stereoscopic view cards which, when seen through the double lenses of a special viewer, jumped into a three-dimensional landscape or scene. They were the forerunner of the Viewmaster and were a prime source of home entertainment. The major manufacturer of these cards was the Kilburn Brothers Stereoscopic View factory in Littleton.

In the bottom level of the Queen Anne–style Town Building (you can't miss its round, white, four-story tower) is the ◆**Historical Museum.** It contains, along with other local artifacts, an exhibition on the Kilburn stereoscopic views. The museum's new Ammonoosuc Room displays local arts and collections, as well as a scale model of the Mount Willard Section House, a Victorian home that once perched beside the tracks in Crawford Notch. The museum is open Wednesdays from 1:30 to 4:30 P.M.; at other times call (603) 444–6586 for information.

Fossils are not common in New Hampshire, and one of the few places where they are found is atop a rock formation overlooking Littleton. The ◈**Kilburn Crags** are the result of great masses of layered, fossil-bearing rock being heaved into an almost vertical position. The fossils aren't just lying about; it takes some effort to find them, but serious geology buffs may find brachipods and ferns here. To reach the crags, continue on Route 118 past the Dells (a pleasant picnic area). Half a mile after it separates from Route 135 in a left turn, look for a sign on the left side of the road with a small pull-out for parking. There is no trail, but you can walk along the edge of the field to an old woods road. Follow it to the top, just over half a mile of steady but not difficult climbing. If fossils don't interest you, the view down over Littleton is worth the climb. Watch for moose, which are plentiful here.

Avoid the interstate here by taking Route 18 to the Connecticut River, which forms both the Vermont border and a huge lake behind ◈**Moore Station Dam.** One of the major power-generating dams in the northeast, it has a visitors' center with displays explaining the dam, as well as a picnic area and boat launch on the reservoir. Write the New England Power Company, North Monroe 03771 or call (603) 638–2327.

Route 135 plays hide-and-seek with the Connecticut River through valley farmland to Woodsville. You can either return to the Littleton area on Route 302 or take Route 112 from Bath to Franconia and Kinsman notches.

In Bath be sure to stop at **The Brick Store,** which has been open in the center of town since 1804. Without being "ye olde general store" about it, this emporium manages to retain the feel and much of the merchandise of an old country store while remaining a useful shopping place for local residents. Top shelves are lined with old tins, a thread cabinet, and other vintage store memorabilia, and the home-made fudge is displayed in a glass case. There's a wheel of cheddar on the counter and four shelves of buffalo-plaid wool shirts, a hot item here in the winter. Notice the slanted counter fronts which make room for hoop skirts. If you stop here for a sandwich (if you don't find one you like in the fridge they'll make one up for you), enjoy it sitting on the front porch with a view of Main Street and the old Mobil sign with the red Pegasus.

Behind the store is the ◈**Bath Village Bridge,** a covered bridge so long that motorists are asked to turn on their headlights when entering it. Built in 1832 at a cost of $3,500, it still has its original arches. Be sure to notice its construction (all covered bridges are not built in the same way), a fine example of a Burr arch structure. At 400 feet, it is the longest in New Hampshire and one of the oldest still in use in America.

Bath has two other covered bridges, one of which is just off Route 112 in the village of Swiftwater. Farther along Route 112 and the Wild Ammonoosuc (don't let this confuse you—there are three different Ammonoosuc rivers in the area), where the road parallels the river for a stretch, there is a spot where hopeful prospectors have had moderate luck panning for gold. You may see their vehicles parked along the road. Route 112 leads to Kinsman Notch.

Northeast of Bath on Route 302 is ◈ **Upper Village,** a cluster of eight homes remarkable enough to make almost anyone ease up on the gas pedal. The most imposing are three grand brick mansions built in the early 1800s. Also set in the carefully manicured grounds, which cover both sides of the road, are other homes and huge, yellow clapboard barns with steep-pitched roofs, all in pristine condition. You expect to see a sign with the name of the museum, but these are private homes. Jeremiah Hutchinson moved to Bath in the winter of 1781 with his wife and twelve children. As you might imagine, it took two sleighs to bring them. There's no place to stop safely, but look as you pass, at this family village of extraordinarily well-preserved Federal-style homes, unlike any other in the state.

Just south of Lisbon, on the east side of the road, is another group of historic homes, although of a much different sort. Early mills frequently provided housing for their workers, whose wages were often too low for them to afford adequate housing on their own. The **company houses** were built in rows, all alike, and called by such names as "Ten Commandments" or "Dirty Dozen." Most of the houses are long gone, but eleven of them stand here in their original row.

Lisbon offers another view of the state, one that you have glimpsed from the hardscrabble farms on the back roads. This is a town with lots of guts and little money, but every year it looks just a little bit more prosperous—another house freshly painted, another porch straightened. They have a Lilac Time Festival toward the end of May. A real hometown event, it has pancake breakfasts, chicken barbecue, races, a golf tournament, quilt show, flea market, crafts, bands, singers, and a Saturday night dance. It's a time of year when summer attractions haven't opened and only the savvy traveler knows it to be a lovely and uncrowded season for a visit. For this year's dates and schedule, write the Lisbon Chamber of Commerce, Lisbon 03585 or call (603) 838–6336.

THE NORTH COUNTRY

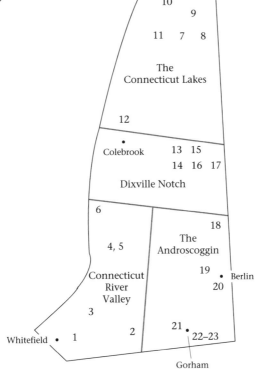

10
9
11 7 8

The
Connecticut Lakes

12

• Colebrook

13 15
14 16 17

Dixville Notch

6

4, 5

The
Androscoggin

18

19 • Berlin
20

Connecticut
River
Valley

3

Whitefield • 1

2

21 •
22–23

Gorham

1. The Spalding Inn
2. Stag Hollow Llama Keep
3. Mount Prospect
4. Nash Stream Watershed
5. Pond Brook Falls
6. The Foolish Frog
7. Coon Brook Valley
8. Garfield Falls
9. Scott Bog and East Inlet
10. Fourth Connecticut Lake
11. The Glen
12. Beaver Brook Falls

13. The Balsams
14. Table Rock
15. The Flume
16. Huntington Cascades
17. Umbagog Lake Campground
18. Thirteen Mile Woods
19. Stone cairns
20. Holy Resurrection Church
21. Moose Brook State Park
22. Gorham Railway Station
23. Moose tours

THE NORTH COUNTRY

The north country isn't for everyone. The nearest mall is hours away; if the local grocery-store-cum-tackle-and-bait shop doesn't have it, you won't need it here. Nightlife consists of swapping fishing or birding stories in front of the fire or soothing muscles tired from canoeing, hiking, or skiing. If there is a Jacuzzi in this part of New Hampshire, it's well hidden.

But if the sight of a moose with a full rack of antlers drinking from a pool at the side of the road makes your heart beat faster, and if the cry of a loon is your favorite song, this is your Serengeti. You'll meet people here with character, not the "ayuh" and hayseed-style characters, but the real stuff. There is a ready wit born of the sense of humor necessary to those who choose the backwoods as a home. It's tent-and-canoe country, with a few fine lodgings for those who prefer their adventures to end in time for a full-course dinner.

Route 3 stays close to the Connecticut River, which at Stewartstown ceases to be the border between New Hampshire and Vermont. Travelers who have seen the Connecticut River flowing through southern New England will hardly recognize this meandering little brook as the same river. Just north of Stewartstown is a sign marking the crossing of the 45th Parallel. From that point north you are closer to the North Pole than to the equator.

CONNECTICUT RIVER VALLEY

No New England golf course has a finer view than the panorama of the White Mountains that spreads out before the greens at the **Mountain View Golf and Country Club.** Overlooking the course from the other side is the vast facade of the Mountain View Hotel, among the last of the big White Mountain resorts. The hotel is empty now and seriously in need of work, but still standing tall, like a dowager who's had to sell her pearls.

Across the street, the clubhouse of the golf course serves lunches daily from 11:00 A.M. to 4:00 P.M. Daily and weekly memberships are offered for the pool, golf course, and tennis courts. Open from May through foliage season, on Mountain View Road in Whitefield; call (603) 837–3885.

A bit farther on down Mountain View Road, ❖ **The Spalding Inn** is at once elegant and informal. First opened in 1926 on the site of an earlier hotel, the inn accommodates guests in the main lodge and in cottages near the pool and tennis courts and in a converted carriage house that was once part of the original hotel. The inn also boasts a fine lawn bowling green; they'll show you how to play. Special arrangements allow guests to use the adjacent Mountain View golf course. The dining room menu changes frequently and might include shrimp with fettucini in a creamy Alfredo sauce or the inn's hallmark dish, filet mignon. Be sure to mention any special diet, since the chef is especially creative in designing alternatives, both at breakfast and dinner. Birders will find binoculars and field guides handy by the terrace window and will enjoy the bird photographs taken by the innkeeper's daughter. Another daughter's paintings decorate the walls of the parlors and the innkeeper herself is responsible for the tasteful decor featuring her own collection of antiques. The Spalding is on Mountain View Road, Whitefield 03598; telephone (603) 837–2572 or (800) 368–VIEW.

A short distance away on Route 116 is Jefferson, an unadorned town set along a ridge facing the mountains. Only the outbuildings remain of the Waumbek Hotel, which once dominated its crossroads, but there are still accommodations in town at **The Jefferson Inn.** A new ell has been added to the original 1896 Victorian house with its tower and wraparound porch, along with woodwork and other architectural detail that either match or fit the style of the original house.

Quilts warm most of the beds, and antiques are mixed with more recent furnishings, creating a nice balance of comfort and style. Families will enjoy the inn's suites and ample recreation space. Couples will find cozy rooms stylishly decorated by the energetic new owners, who have added a historical theme and their personal art collection. Reasonably priced, the inn is open all year except for April and November. Write The Jefferson Inn, Route 2, Jefferson 03583 or call (603) 586–7998 or (800) 729–7908.

If you are tired of carrying your camera bags and your bird guides on your autumn explorations into the national forest, go to ❖**Stag Hollow Llama Keep.** Their llamas will carry packs on half- or full-day treks on White Mountain trails. The treks take you through seldom-traveled trails tailored to your own interests, such as local history (complete with ghost villages and cellar holes) or woodland flora. Treks are offered only in the fall. Write Stag Hollow, R.F.D. 1, Jefferson 03583; call (603) 586–4598 after 5:00 P.M.

Close by is the northern end of the road over Jefferson Notch (see p. 108), in case you decide to travel it from this direction. The road is well marked from the Jefferson end.

Just before reaching Lancaster, Route 2 passes over a shoulder of ◆**Mount Prospect,** a low peak easily spotted because of the stone tower at its summit. The tower and the stone-and-stucco "lodge" beside it were built by a man to whom the north country and everyone who travels there owes a tremendous debt. John Wingate Weeks was a U.S. senator and cabinet member to two presidents, but is remembered most as the father of the White Mountain National Forest. It was the "Weeks Law" that authorized the government to buy and preserve forest areas in the east.

The tower and buildings are now in a state park encompassing 420 acres on the mountain. The lodge contains an outstanding collection of local birds, historical displays on the White Mountains, and a gallery of photographs that reflect Mr. Weeks's prominent role in world affairs and the friends who visited the estate. Free lectures on historical and ecological topics are held at the lodge on Thursday evenings throughout the summer. The lodge and tower are open from 10:00 A.M. to 6:00 P.M. Tuesday through Sunday from mid-June until Labor Day; from Memorial Day until mid-June and Labor Day through mid-October, they are open weekends only. For a current schedule of evening programs call (603) 788–4004 or 788–3155.

Farther north, just before Route 3 reaches Groveton, Route 110 branches to the right (east) and travels along the upper Ammonoosuc River. To the north lies the ◆**Nash Stream Watershed,** an area whose future has been the subject of an intense battle among land developers, the state, and several conservation groups. Forty thousand acres of it have finally been secured as public lands, a mixed habitat for hawks, falcons, and smaller birds in a forested valley. Access is via Emerson Road, about 2 miles east of Groveton. Follow it another 2 miles to a fork, and then go left. After about 4.5 miles of dirt road, a right fork leads uphill to Little Pond Bog, a fine spot for fly fishing high above the valley. In the winter this area is crisscrossed by cross-country ski trails.

If you continue straight ahead less than half a mile instead of taking the right, you come to ◈**Pond Brook Falls,** a series of waterfalls known to very few people outside of Groveton and Stark. Just after crossing a culvert you will see a pull-out area to the right. Park there and follow the trail a short distance to the lower falls (watch for moose tracks—this is a favorite path for them, too). You'll hear the falls before you see them, and then you'll see only part of them. Continuing uphill, the path ends at a second falls; from here the best route is over the sloping granite ledge alongside the rushing water. Except during spring runoff, there is plenty of room on this 50-foot-wide span of rock for both you and the brook.

Keep going upstream for an ever-changing series of falls, some gushing through narrow chutes and others spread in a filmy veil across a wide ledge. As you reach the top of each, you look up to see another of different size and shape. This is New Hampshire's sampler of waterfall styles. Do be careful after a rain or in the early spring when the rocks are wet, since they can be quite slippery to climb. On wet days, go through the woods next to the falls where the footing is more secure.

Back on Route 110, continue on to visit Stark, a mountain town clustered around its covered bridge under Devil's Slide, a 700-foot precipice. During World War II, Stark housed a **camp for German prisoners of war.** The remarkable story of how these men, taken prisoner in North Africa, became friends of local farmers during their long winters together is told in *Stark Decency* by Allen Koop. East of the village, on Route 110, a state sign marks the site of the camp, where only cellar holes remain.

The well-kept house with a terrace overlooking the river, just over the covered bridge in Stark, is the **Stark Village Inn Bed and Breakfast,** offering three antiques-furnished guest rooms and a great deal of homey comfort to travelers. Hiking, canoeing, fishing, climbing, cross-country skiing, and bicycling begin at the doorstep of this restored farmhouse, and photographers could spend the day sitting on the front porch capturing the river and the bridge in all their different moods and lights. A full country breakfast is cooked on the big black woodstove in the kitchen; in summer guests can eat on the terrace overlooking the river. Low rates make this a bargain as well as a treat. Write to them at R.F.D. 1, Box 389, Groveton 03582 or call (603) 636–2644.

Rock hounds take note: At Diamond Ledge on Long Mountain and also on the south slope of Percy Peak, about 200 feet below the summit, amethyst is found in the surface rock; topaz is found at Diamond Ledge. You will need to get thorough directions locally or use a topographic map.

On the last Sunday of each June, dozens of fiddlers gather in Stark for the **Old Time Fiddlers Contest** at Whitcomb Field. Bring the whole family, lawn chairs, and a picnic lunch or buy your lunch there. Admission is charged. Call (603) 636–1325 for details.

Groveton is a paper mill town, although the enormous piles of pulpwood, the logjams in the river, and the terrible smell that once characterized it are long gone. Here are a covered bridge, painted white, and a vintage logging steam locomotive near the main intersection. **McKenzie's Diner** on Route 3 just north of town serves generous portions, homemade fries, and good breakfasts. They are open seven days a week, 5:30 A.M. to 8:00 P.M.

Between the towns of Stratford and North Stratford, on the right, look for ◆ **The Foolish Frog.** This unexpected roadside museum is the personal twenty-five-year collection of Carol Hawley and Francis McMilleon, housing hundreds upon hundreds of frogs made of every conceivable material and in every imaginable style. Along with frog whatsits and gimcracks there are fine folk art sculptures including an Indonesian frog deity, a frog flute from Colombia, a rubber frog from the Amazon, plus pottery, baskets, puzzles, bottle stoppers, batiks, mechanical banks, puppets, and potholders. It is fascinating to see how a creature common throughout the world has been adapted as a design motif in so many ways. A small shelf in the center of the room displays frogs for sale, including several unique wooden toys. There is no admission charge, but there is a discreet little box for donations, which help to keep the collection growing. The Foolish Frog is open from May through foliage season, but there are no set hours. Write RR#1, Box 428, Route 3, North Stratford 03590 or call (603) 636–1887.

THE CONNECTICUT LAKES

The town of Pittsburg is geographically the largest in New Hampshire, over 20 miles wide and covering more than 360 square miles. The entire tip of New Hampshire, from the Maine to Vermont borders to the international border with Canada, lies within its boundaries. The whole town was an independent nation for three years beginning in 1832. Claimed by both New Hampshire and Canada, and with no decisive action taken by either to settle the issue, the Indian Stream Territory was left in chronic limbo. Tiring of this, and not wishing to be governed by either contender, the citizens voted their independence at a town meeting. This finally brought them to everyone's attention. After three years and a few altercations among the local militia, a Canadian sheriff's posse, and a small company of New Hampshire militia, the Republic of Indian Stream became the town of Pittsburg.

Within Pittsburg's borders lie all four of the Connecticut Lakes and Lake Francis, and mile after mile of forests, mountain streams, bogs, and assorted wilderness lands. Pittsburg's main (almost its only) road borders each lake in turn until it finally climbs the "height-of-land" to the Canadian border station. ("Height-of-land" is a term commonly used in the north country to describe the high point of any of the area's many ridges.) At nearly any point you may see deer or moose by the roadside.

What is unique here is the series of pristine water bodies. Uninhabited by man, these provide habitat for wild shorebirds found in few other places. Loon populations are increasing here. You can put in a canoe on nearly any pond, and you are welcome to roam the woods roads built by the timber companies as long as they are not barred. The whole area abounds with trout.

◆ **Coon Brook Valley,** a long, wide, marshy area cut by a woods road, is a sure place to see moose at almost any time of day. To find it, look for a road marked MAGALLOWAY TOWER entering Route 3 from the right. Go a few yards north and take the road entering from the opposite side of Route 3. Just drive in and park in an open spot—you may even see moose before you park.

For an adventure into the outer reaches of the wilderness, but one that requires only a short hike, search out ◆ **Garfield Falls.** Take the above-mentioned gravel road marked MAGALLOWAY TOWER, following the tower signs until you reach the height of land. At this point a dirt road to the tower goes off to the right, but you should keep going. About 2 miles after you pass Paradise Camp on your left, you will go down a hill and see a road bearing off to the right (the road straight ahead of you may be blocked just below this). Follow the road to the right $1\frac{1}{10}$ mile to where it

Coon Brook Valley

makes a sharp left turn and crosses a bridge. Take the dirt road right at the turn.

It's narrow, but unless there have been heavy rains, it is easily passable without four-wheel drive. In another $1\frac{1}{10}$ mile the road opens out into a yard (an open area where logs are stored). Park there and look for a trail into the woods on the left side of the road. It may take a few minutes to find it if there have been logging operations there recently, but it is just to the right of a tree with several small forest signs on it, close by a tumble of large rocks.

Garfield Falls is only a five-minute walk from here, through a forest carpeted in the spring with trillium, clintonia, bunchberry, wood sorrel, and occasional moose droppings that look like piles of nutmegs beside (or in) the trail. The falls will be to your left, dropping off the facing side of a chasm into a pool almost directly under your feet. It comes through a zigzag shoot and then bounces off the boulder with such force that it has worn a depression in the face of the cliff as well as a cave at its base where its velocity creates a whirlpool. Below the falls the river is split by a giant boulder from which you can get an excellent view of the falls—and the deeply undercut bank that you were just standing on!

This is not a trip to begin with bald tires, with a near-empty gas tank, or in a downpour of rain, but it is quite an easy one. The distances aren't great, just slow to cover. Before you curse the timber companies for their cutting throughout this area, remember two points. First, you are traveling on their roads, which are the only access to these areas in case of forest fires. Second, their cutting, done with the techniques that they now employ, creates a far more inviting habitat for birds and animals than dense forest provides.

A little farther up Route 3, just above Second Connecticut Lake, another timber road to the right leads to ◆**Scott Bog and East Inlet.** The road curves down into a valley and across a stream to a rough T, where you should go left to find Scott Bog or right to find East Inlet. The latter is a former log drive impoundment from which logs were floated out on the spring thaw. In 1987, Champion Paper Company donated 426 acres of pristine pond and moose pasture here, including a tract of virgin spruce and fir, to the Nature Conservancy. The Scott Bog-East Inlet area is considered by birders to offer the best sightings in the north country, with spruce grouse, Canada jay, sixteen warbler varieties, and the rare black-backed woodpecker. Sightings of eighty to ninety species in three days are quite common here.

Wandering around on these woods roads is a lot easier and less nerve-wracking with the inexpensive map "Roads and Trails, Connecticut Lake Region" printed on waterproof paper and available at most stores in the area.

The Connecticut River, barely a trickle now, crosses the road above Second Connecticut Lake, and the tiny **Deer Mountain Campground** sits on its northern banks. Its twenty campsites are rustic: No hot showers, flush toilets, or camp store here, but there is plenty of quiet and the riverbanks are alive with birds. The **Moose Falls Flowage,** just north of the campground, is a good place to put in a canoe. The campground is open from May until the end of October.

133

Third Connecticut Lake has a boat ramp right off Route 3, but ◆ **Fourth Connecticut Lake** takes a bit more effort. Only about an acre in size, it is reached by a trail from the U.S. Customs station at the Canadian border. The trail, which is actually the cleared swath along the border, is "steep and rugged," as the map warns. Because it is rocky, it is not a hike for street shoes. Park and sign in at the customs station, where they will give you a trail map. It is only about ½ mile to the seventy-five–acre site that Champion Paper Company donated to the Nature Conservancy in 1990. Be sure to walk around the upper part of the lake to find the spot where the first few drops of the mighty Connecticut River trickle from the rocks.

The best way to enjoy this area is to settle in for a few days, and the best place to do that is in a comfortable log cabin or lodge overlooking a lake. ◆ **The Glen,** a former private estate, looks as though it had grown there with the tall spruce trees that line the shores of First Connecticut Lake. The big lodge, which has been welcoming guests for more than thirty years, is a convivial place with a huge stone fireplace and comfortable Adirondack log and maple furniture; you can also opt for the seclusion of your own cabin. The atmosphere here is comfortable, not cute. There are no frilly curtains or designer sheets, but you won't be roughing it either.

All meals are included in the rate, and they'll pack you a box lunch; they will even fill your thermos with hot coffee when you leave for your day's adventure. Dinners in the dining room are generous, including such entrées as haddock filet with shrimps and scallops, served with vegetables, pilaf, and wine. The whipped cream on your chocolate cream pie is real, and the vegetables in the salad bar are crisp and fresh. Meals prepared to suit special diets are treated with the same careful attention.

The tone and warmth of The Glen is set by its owner, Betty Falton. She helps guests choose places to hike, fish, bird, or just wander around, suggesting routes and telling about her own favorite nooks and crannies. Betty keeps rental boats moored on various lakes so you won't have to haul them around, or you can bring your own. She loves her "neighborhood," but she stresses that this is not the place for everyone's taste. "If you can't walk to the brook without seeing something interesting, you don't belong here," she is quick to tell prospective guests.

When the full moon rises over Mount Magalloway, reflecting in the lake and outlining the spiky silhouettes of the fir trees around the lake, it looks like the stage set for *Rose Marie*. If the lure of the wilderness charms you, there's no finer place to enjoy it. The Glen is open from mid-May to October, when you can call for reservations at (603) 538–6500. From December to April call Betty at (508) 475–0559, or call (800) 445–GLEN.

While The Glen serves meals to non-guests by reservation, you can also get a good breakfast, lunch, or dinner at the **Midtown Restaurant.** It may look a little tired on the outside, but this family-run restaurant serves well-prepared meals. Fries are home-made, sandwiches generous, and the clam roll overflows with whole clams. When you ask for a glass of milk here, it comes ice-cold and in a sixteen-ounce tumbler. Open every day except Wednesday, year-round.

South of Pittsburg you have a choice of roads. Route 145 covers the same route, but in a straighter line. At least on the map it's straighter—if you ironed out the hills, the length would probably be the same. The view from the hilltops, past hillside farms and forests to the skyline of mountains to the south, makes it a nice change from Route 3's river-bottom route.

❖ **Beaver Brook Falls** drops almost onto Route 145, about 2½ miles before you reach Colebrook. You will see small parking areas on both sides of the road before you see the falls. Be pre-pared for a surprise, especially if it has rained recently—somehow one doesn't expect the 35-foot straight drop of a waterfall to appear out of the woods, particularly on the side of the road. Below, a series of cascades spill from pool to pool. At the foot of the falls is a small park with picnic tables and a swimming hole. If you aren't going into the tip of the state, you can get to the falls via Route 145 out of Colebrook (the sign is marked CLARKSVILLE), making the 5-mile side trip before going on to Dixville Notch.

DIXVILLE NOTCH

Unlike most of New Hampshire's other notches, which run north and south, Dixville lies east and west. Route 26 follows the Mohawk River all the way from Colebrook to the notch itself. About 3 miles outside of Colebrook, look for East Colebrook Road going up the hill to your left. The road continues upward giving fine views over the notch. At the intersection by an old school-house, a left will bring you to a unique lodging, **Rooms with a View.** Unlike most New Hampshire bed and breakfasts, this one is in a newly-built home, set in a hilltop meadow with its porch rockers overlooking the Connecticut Valley and Dixville Notch. The kitchen is in the center of the house, and you are welcome to watch Sonja bake her bread (fresh every day and sweetened with her own honey) in the huge Tulikivi soapstone stove that domi-nates the room. Or you can just sit in the bright dining room and enjoy the view while she serves you a full, made-from-scratch country breakfast.

Each room is different, with a graceful mix of antique and new furniture. Beds are warmed by quilts pieced by Sonja, and each bathroom has a fuzzy, thick sheepskin mat. The house was built to share, and it's a warm and welcoming place to come home to after your north country travels. Moderately priced and open year-round, for reservations write Rooms with a View, R. R. #1, Forbes Road, Colebrook 03576 or call (603) 237–5106 or (800) 499–5106.

For many visitors, the goal and the reward of the long trip to this far-off tip of the state is staying at the world-class grand hotel set just below the head of the notch. ◆ **The Balsams** is unique in so many ways that we'll mention only a few. Once one of many large resort hotels where city families came to spend the summer before the days of air conditioning, The Balsams is still thriving, having weathered the tough financial climates as well as it has weathered its natural climate. It has turned the harsh win-ters to advantage by opening a family ski area and miles of cross-country ski trails, keeping Lake Gloriette open for skating, giving snowshoe lessons, and offering the free use of snowshoes.

Their success is even more surprising because of the hotel's remote location, but therein lies another unique feature. Unlike the other big hotels that were built in the busy White Mountain circuit, The Balsams stands alone, with none of the tourist attrac-tions of the more heavily-traveled routes. It is a gracious and highly civilized oasis in a vast wilderness, and its owners have turned that fact to their advantage. They have provided so many activities, sporting opportunities, social events, and gastronomic pleasures that it would take a week to enjoy them all. In the sum-mer, there are golf, hiking, walks with a staff naturalist, fishing in the lakes and streams, boating, canoeing, tennis, moose watching, swimming, dancing, movies, cooking lessons, a daily sports program, and the opportunity just to sit on the wide veranda and look at the mountains.

One of the few resorts operating on the American plan, The Balsams includes all meals in the room rate, and you won't want to miss one. Breakfast and lunch are offered as buffets with service, and always make for an impressive production rich in variety. Lunch brings an entire table of mouth-watering desserts, of which you are welcome to sample as many as your appetite allows. Dinner is more formal, with a wide choice of entrées as elegant and innovative or as traditional as you like. A sauté of scallops and shrimp with ginger and cilantro, veal Oscar, broiled tuna with a citrus butter sauce, venison loin with wild mushrooms, or pecan roasted pork may be among the several nightly choices. This is not the usual hotel dining room fare, and this top-quality cuisine is one of the primary reasons for the success of the entire resort. Another reason is the warm and personal service in the dining room and elsewhere in the hotel.

Did we mention that The Balsams welcomes families and provides special activities, ski programs, and babysitting so that parents can enjoy some time to themselves as well? While there, don't miss **Tilly's Balloons,** the factory store for the local industry, where you can choose from a rainbow assortment of balloons displayed in jars, as in a jelly bean store. Or the room where the residents of Dixville gather every four years at midnight to cast the nation's first ballots for the presidential election. Write The Balsams, Dixville Notch 03576; call (603) 255–3400 or (800) 255–0800 in New Hampshire or (800) 255–0600 elsewhere.

Between meals at The Balsams, explore the notch. You can vary your level of exercise, beginning with a walk around the Lake Gloriette walking trail, a 1.4-mile loop, with the hotel's *Natural History Handbook* as your guide. This informative little book explains the geology of the notch and helps you identify its abundant wildflowers and birds. More energy is required for the climb up to ◆**Table Rock,** especially if you take the rock-strewn trail that goes almost straight up from the notch. A more gentle ascent can be made by a trail beginning near the Balsam/Wilderness Ski Area entrance road. Table Rock overlooks The Balsams, the lake, and the notch, but it's no place for an acrophobic.

137

At the point where the trail drops steeply to Table Rock, another trail leads away from the ledges. If you follow it for a few yards you will come to a deep split in the rock face. This **Ice Chasm** has snow and ice in it even during the hottest summer days. Although there is no sign leading to it, you won't have trouble finding it; you just have to know it is there. Be careful: It can be dangerous if you get too close to the sharp edge. A new trail in progress from Huntington Cascades to Table Rock makes a complete circuit through the notch opening up new views.

After hiking, be sure to stop for a refreshing drink of pure mountain spring water at the newly-built **Spring House,** an exact reproduction of the original, which was a popular destination for a Sunday "drive." Many locals remember the spring as the scene of their first kiss or even the place of their marriage proposal. There must be something about the water!

If you want to know where to buy hand-tied flies, hire a good fishing guide, find Mable Sims's fish pond, or rent a canoe, ask Ray Gorman, the chief concierge at The Balsams. He's an experienced outdoorsman and a native of the area, the perfect concierge for such a resort. He can also tell you about the "lonesome loon" in the lake.

❖ **The Flume** is on the other side of the notch, and on your way there you can appreciate how wild this notch is compared to Franconia, Pinkham, and even Crawford notches. It's a *real* notch, where you go over a hump in the road, through a cleft in the cliffs, and down a steep, winding road squeezed between two tree-covered walls. The difference is geological: The surface rock here has been tilted on end so that its strata stand upright, causing the craggy eroded points of rock that give it such a wild aspect.

About a mile past the head of the notch look for a picnic area on the left. The geology changes back to granite here, as Flume Brook carves a gorge more than 200 feet long with sides so straight it almost seems to have been built from cut blocks of stone. It is 40 feet deep in places, as the brook drops from pool to pool and finally over the edge of a ledge. Walk along the rim, and in the spring look for trillium and white and pink lady's slippers beside the trail. They are protected species, so enjoy them in place.

Just a few yards down Route 26, this time on the right, is the road to a second picnic area. ❖ **Huntington Cascades** is reached by a short path to the brook and then a short walk upstream. The falls continue above the one that you can see from the base, but there is no trail up the steep slope beside the falls, so most visitors simply enjoy the lower section as it rushes in its curving path over the rocks. If you do go exploring here, be careful and stay away from the edge, which has been undercut by the brook. In case you wondered, the little cemetery by the entrance to the parking area contains the remains of some of the area's earliest settlers.

The 5 miles of road between Huntington Cascades and the town of Errol is a prime stretch for moose viewing, so drive slowly and keep watch. You can't miss the Errol International Airport, whose building is so tiny that its long name has to be abbreviated to fit across its facade.

Each of the two roads leaving from the far end of Errol's main street will take you to the Maine border. Route 16, to the left, offers a pleasant drive along the upper Androscoggin and the Magalloway rivers. Route 26 leads to the southern shores of **Lake Umbagog** and one of the most beautiful and unusual campgrounds in all of New England.

Lake Umbagog is a wildlife sanctuary, with one of the nation's largest loon nesting areas. Bald eagles have also nested there for several years, raising chicks of their own and even a chick from an adopted egg from New York State. Other bird life and, of course, moose abound. ✦**Umbagog Lake Campground** is, like most of this north country, not for everyone. "We cater to canvas," says owner Jim Willard, by which he means that they will accommodate your RV if they have room, but the campground is really designed for tents. Along with sites overlooking the length of Umbagog's blue waters, the shady wooded sites and the handful of cottages, there are more than thirty wilderness campsites on islands or shores of the lake without road access. The farthest of these is 11 miles from the campground; Jim will take you to your site by motorboat if you don't want to paddle all the way. You can bring your own rowboat or canoe, or rent theirs, for exploring the lake.

These sites are isolated, at least a half-mile apart, some on islands. They are not for beginning campers, but for the woods wise and the water wise they offer real camping that is very hard to find. Open from Memorial Day to mid-September; you can reserve sites. Write Umbagog Lake Campground, P.O. Box 181, Errol 03579; call (603) 482–7795.

139

In Errol, **Saco Bound** rents canoes and kayaks, as well as operating a full transportation service so you can put in at one place and be picked up at a different location. In the summer they offer reasonably-priced guided day trips complete with a barbecue lunch. They operate a whitewater canoe and kayak school at Errol, as well as a campground for their customers. Write Saco Bound, Box 119, Center Conway 03813; call (603) 447–2177 or 447–3801.

THE ANDROSCOGGIN

South of Errol on Route 16 begins a scenic stretch where the road and the Androscoggin River travel side by side through ◆ **Thirteen Mile Woods.** The river is wide and for the most part gentle, and there are put-ins at several different points. If you have ever held a paddle, you will long to be on the water in this flat reach where the trees overhang the water. There is even a campground, the Mollidgewock, right on the river and designed primarily for canoeists. It is open from mid-May to December 1. Be sure to call them at (603) 482–3373 to reserve a site, since its half-mile frontage on calm water and rapids is a favorite teaching area for groups learning whitewater techniques.

Motorists will find good places for a riverside picnic, or to just sit and watch the river traffic go by. Below the Thirteen Mile Woods is another area frequented by moose, where it is not unusual to see them beside (or in) the road.

North of Berlin look for the ◆ **stone cairns** in the river, among the last reminders of the days of the logging drives that were common in this country during the nineteenth and early twentieth centuries. These mid-river cairns served as the point from which the great chain booms were secured. These captured and held a vast flotilla of logs during the annual spring release of the timber that had been harvested during the winter. As trees were cut during the winter, the logs were hauled into impoundment ponds. During the runoff, the dams holding these ponds were released. The water and logs in it broke into a wild frenzy of energy and wood that found its way downstream into the sawmills and paper plants of New England.

Berlin (pronounced with the accent on the first syllable) is a paper mill town; you can't miss the smokestacks of the James River Corporation. It has been a paper town ever since the first

Holy Resurrection Church

logging camp was established in 1825, although the first paper mill didn't open until 1852. At one time, it was estimated that the paper produced in Berlin annually would cover a road 15 feet wide that would run nineteen times around the world. The mill brought immigrants from Canada and as far away as Russia. These ethnic groups have mixed and moved, but a few traces remain from the days when church services in the community were conducted in five different languages.

Saint Anne's church, a classic French-Canadian brick structure, rises like a fortress in the center of town, enormously tall, with an oversized statue on top. But far more unexpected is ◆ **Holy Resurrection Church.** Take Mount Forist Street, which intersects with Main Street near the post office, and follow it up the hill. When we say *up*, we mean almost straight up what may well be New Hampshire's steepest street. Just before the street ends, go left on Russian Street, still going uphill, and look to your right. Six polished, gold-leafed, onion-shaped domes crown a gem of a Russian Orthodox church on the corner of Petrograd Street. Each dome is surmounted by a double patriarchal gold cross; the rest of the church is white. It sits above the city overlooking the smokestacks and rows of company housing below, a poignant and rare reminder of the homesickness of the many peoples that were propelled into this strange and new land.

For a fine view over the mountains to the west, take the **Cates Hill Scenic Route,** turning right off High Street onto Hillside Avenue. The road continues to climb until it reaches a ridge of cleared meadows with a backdrop of mountains. You can reach Hillside Avenue from Route 16 north of town by taking the road marked "Coos County Home" and continuing to the top of the hill.

On Jimtown Road, just off of Route 5 west of Gorham, is a very pleasant campground at **Moose Brook State Park.** Its forty-six sites are well-spaced in open forest, with a few at the edge of a field. An ingenious warming pool brings the icy-cold waters of Moose Brook up to a more suitable temperature before it flows into the swimming pool downstream. There is a picnic area near the swimming pool. Be sure to notice the architecture of the administration building, which is a classic of Civilian Conservation Corps (CCC) construction. The park is open from late May through Labor Day. It is not possible to reserve campsites, but you can call (603) 466–3860 for information.

Across from the Town Hall on the Common in Gorham, the Victorian **Railway Station** has been turned into a museum by the local historical society. The collection emphasizes the years when the railway was the lifeblood of the region, but contains other memorabilia as well, including a stereoscope visitors can actually use to view the collection of historic cards. Hours vary; call (603) 466–5570.

While in Gorham, inquire at the information booth about **moose tours** sponsored by the Chamber of Commerce. These take visitors by van to some of the most likely locations for spotting moose, showing a video about the local logging heritage on the way. The tour leaves the information booth on the common at sunset daily from mid-May through Columbus Day weekend. Call (603) 466–3103 or 752–6060.

At the corner of Gorham's town green opposite the railroad station, the meticulously restored **Gorham House B&B** adorns the main street with its painted wood trim, wide porch, and round tower. Inside, the rooms are period pieces, with just enough Victoriana to keep them interesting. The Inn is at 55 Main Street (P.O. Box 267), Gorham 03581; call 466–2271.

While the Old Man of The Mountains, in Franconia Notch, is the state's best known symbol, **The Old Man of the Valley** in Shelburne is virtually unknown. This will most likely change now that a modest sign has appeared on the south side of Route 2 between Gorham and the Maine border. Park in the pull-out just east of the sign. Walk back to the sign, where a short trail enters the woods. A short distance ahead is a large stone with the profile of a man on one side. Surely, you say, this has just been sculpted to look this way, but a walk around the stone shows a jumble of perfectly natural planes that form the face when viewed from the front.

A NOTE ABOUT OUR LESS APPEALING WILDLIFE

While May's lilacs are safe as the state's flower, there is talk every spring about changing the state bird from the purple finch (which we rarely see) to the mosquito or blackfly, which we see all too often. Unless you have allergies to their bites, these springtime insects are merely an annoyance. They don't carry malaria or yellow fever as their tropical relatives do, and slapping them is a source of moderate exercise.

But in the north country, especially in May and June, it is wise to be prepared with long sleeves, long pants, and shirts with collars when these voracious creatures are at their worst—evenings and mornings and in the deep woods.

Everyone has a favorite brand of repellent; we favor Natrapel for most places, the only repellent we know of with EPA approval and that comes in a propellant-free spray and a recyclable bottle. Natrapel is a New Hampshire product, created by people who know mosquitos and black flies intimately. For sources call (800) 258–4696 or write Tender Corp., P.O. Box 290, Littleton 03561.

INDEX

144

145